A THEOI Y

of CHA

A New Perspectiv vil,
and Suff

ELYSIA Mc
SAFHI JAI

5 Fold Media
Visit us at www.5foldmedia.com

A Theology of Chaos
Copyright © 2014 by Elysia McColley and Safhi Jai
Published by 5 Fold Media, LLC
www.5foldmedia.com

Unless otherwise identified, Scripture quotations are taken from the NEW AMERICAN STANDARD BIBLE®, Copyright © 1960,1962,1963,1968,1971,1972,1973,1975,1977,1995 by The Lockman Foundation. Used by permission.

Scripture quotations marked NKJV are taken from the New King James Version. Copyright © 1982 by Thomas Nelson, Inc. Used by permission. All rights reserved.

All emphasis within Scripture quotations is the author's own.

ISBN: 978-1-936578-87-0
Library of Congress Control Number: 2014930217

He has made everything beautiful in its time.
Also He has put eternity in their hearts, except
that no one can find out the work that God does
from beginning to end.

-Ecclesiastes 3:11 NKJV

Contents

Prologue   7

Part 1: When Life Doesn't Make Sense

    Chapter 1: The Problem of Suffering   11

    Chapter 2: Biblical Responses to the Problem of Suffering   17

    Chapter 3: Chaos Theory   23

    Chapter 4: What Went Wrong   29

    Chapter 5: Chaos and the Kingdom of Darkness   35

Part 2: A Heavenly Perspective

    Chapter 6: A New Perspective   43

    Chapter 7: A Biblical View of God in Suffering   49

    Chapter 8: Our Great High Priest   59

    Chapter 9: The Message of Jesus   65

Part 3: Kingdom Chaos

    Chapter 10: The Unstoppable Kingdom   73

    Chapter 11: Chaos and the Kingdom   81

    Chapter 12: Evil for Good   89

    Chapter 13: Evil and the Glory of God   97

    Chapter 14: Redemption   103

    Chapter 15: The Grander Design   113

Part 4: Our Response to Evil and Suffering

    Chapter 16: Partnering With God   121

    Chapter 17: What Now? Practical Steps to Finding God in
          Chaos   129

Prologue

Thousands of years ago, east of Israel in the land that is now the kingdom of Jordan, there lived a very wealthy man named Job. He had seven sons and three daughters, as well as seven thousand sheep, three thousand camels, five hundred yoke of oxen, five hundred donkeys, and many servants.

Job was very righteous in the eyes of God. One day Satan came before the Lord, and the Lord said to him, "Have you considered My servant Job? There is no one on earth like him. He is blameless and upright, a man who fears God and stays away from evil."

Satan responded, "The only reason Job fears You is because You have put a hedge of protection around him and his household and everything he has. You have blessed the work of his hands, so that his flocks and herds are spread throughout the land. But stretch out Your hand and destroy everything he has, and he will surely curse You to Your face."

God replied, "Very well then. Everything he has is in your hands, but on Job himself do not lay a finger."

One day one of Job's servants came running to him, bringing a horrifying report. "Calamity has struck!" he said. "Your oxen were plowing your fields and the donkeys were grazing nearby. Then the Sabeans came and attacked. They killed all of your servants and carried off all of your livestock. I am the only one who escaped to tell you!"

Before the news had the chance to settle in, another servant ran in. "Calamity has struck! The fire of God fell from the sky and burned up your sheep and your servants who were taking care of them. I, only I, managed to escape to tell you!"

A Theology of Chaos

Barely had the words left his lips when another servant ran in. "Calamity has struck! Raiders from the north, the Chaldeans, came down and carried off all of your camels. They killed all of the servants, except that I alone escaped to tell you!"

Before he had finished telling his report another servant ran in, bearing the worst news of all. "Your sons and daughters were at the oldest brother's house, feasting and drinking wine. A strong desert wind came and struck the house. It collapsed and killed everyone inside. All ten of your children are dead."

Job stood up and tore his robe and shaved his head. Then he fell to the ground and worshiped God, saying, "The Lord gives and the Lord takes away. Blessed be the name of the Lord!"

On another day Satan came before the Lord again. The Lord again commended Job to him for his righteousness, saying that even though he was brought to ruin, there was no one on earth like him.

Satan responded, saying, "That is because You have not allowed me to harm the man himself. But watch and see; a man will do anything to preserve his own life. When his flesh and bones are afflicted, he will surely curse You to Your face."

"Do with him as you please," said the Lord. "Only you may not take his life."

Job was afflicted with painful sores, from the bottom of his feet to the top of his head. He sat down in ashes with a piece of broken pottery and scraped his sores.

In reading the book of Job, we must realize that suffering does not necessarily have a formula or a direct cause. God allowed His faithful servant to endure severe hardships before delivering him. God did this, at the beginning, to prove Job to Satan. Yet, at the end of the book, we see that all along God was really proving Himself to Job.

Part 1: When Life Doesn't Make Sense

Chapter 1: The Problem of Suffering

Rachel was born to parents who never wanted a daughter. At least, they did not want her. Her earliest memory, from when she was two years old, is of her mother beating her with a two by four until she was on the ground. Repeated beatings such as this one over the next few years left her with excruciating scoliosis. As a young child, her parents repeatedly left her home by herself; when she was three, somebody broke in and raped her. But the police were never called. Instead, her mother's response was to take away the rest of her dignity by cutting off all of her thick, curly hair, as if to show Rachel that now she could never be beautiful. She was raped again when she was five—this time by her best friend's teenage half-brother. Again, the police were not called; this time her mother responded by putting her on a diet, again letting her know just how unlovely she really was. From kindergarten on, her mother would starve her to try to force her to lose weight.

When Rachel was eleven years old, her dad drove her to a children's home, dropped her off, and left. After four years of experiencing all kinds of trauma and abuse in foster care, a judge sent her back to her parents. A few weeks and several beatings later, her dad told her, with nothing short of demonic rage in his eyes, that he wanted to beat her so badly that she would be in the hospital, and that he would gladly go to prison for it. At one point, he backed her into a corner, grabbed her by her neck, and held her with her feet off the ground.

C.S. Lewis was one of the most brilliant biblical thinkers of the twentieth century. Over half a century after his death, his works still greatly influence western Christianity. But from age fifteen, despite being raised in a Christian home, he was a self-professed atheist. One reason why his atheism continued well into adulthood was the horror he faced in the trenches as a soldier during World War I. In the opening pages of his book, *The Problem of Pain,* Lewis concisely summed up a question with which many of us are confronted all too often: If God is entirely powerful, and entirely good, then why do bad things happen?[1]

Many of you have probably asked the same question. Because the fact is that we live in a world where one billion people live on less than one dollar a day, and every single minute 15 children die from something related to poverty:—starvation, dehydration, or a preventable disease. There are 200 million orphans in the world today, with 500,000 residing in foster homes in America. Every single day in America, fifty people die from a drunk driving accident, and three children die from child abuse. One third of all girls and one sixth of all boys in America are sexually abused before the age of 18. And yet the Bible tells us to believe that God is good.

Rachel and I are very good friends, and her story provides much insight into the question of God, evil, and suffering. In high school, she became a believer. She read the Bible diligently, along with many books on Christianity, and in college she majored in theology, because she wanted to understand the problem of suffering. She wanted to know why so many terrible things had happened to her. She wanted to somehow rationalize something that was completely irrational. Instead, she realized that she didn't want answers. She wanted to be rescued; she wanted her suffering to end. She also found that there are no easy answers, and there is no going back and erasing the past.

Thank God not everybody has a story like Rachel's, but suffering is a universal experience. You don't have to be in circumstances as extreme as Rachel's to be suffering. You don't even have to be in a dire place. I have met many women—incredibly beautiful women—who look in the mirror and don't see anything special. They would give anything to feel beautiful. Plenty of extremely intelligent people think that they don't measure up because their gift does not lie in another area. They may not be traumatized, but they are still suffering.

---

1. C.S. Lewis *The Problem of Pain* (London: The Centenary Press, 1940).

The experience of suffering also doesn't need to be something happening right now. Many times we don't even realize that we are suffering from something that happened a long time ago, such as a past trauma or the loss of someone close. I'm not trying to encourage people to throw pity parties for things that happened in the past. But I do want those of you who are reading this to be honest with yourself and with God about where you are and where you are going, as well as the things that may be hindering your relationship with Him.

Why?

No one word seems to sum up a person's response to suffering better than, "Why?" Why me? Why did this happen? Why did You take my child? Why am I now in a wheelchair? I did everything right! I fed the homeless; I went to church; I followed the Ten Commandments. I even taught Sunday school and vacation Bible school and went on mission trips! How could You let this happen? Why did You do this to me?

My nephew is now two years old—right at the age where he is trying to explore as much of the world as he possibly can. A few weeks ago he discovered that cell phones don't go down the toilet when you flush. Being exceptionally bright, after getting a spanking for attempting to flush his mom's cell phone, he asked, "Why it not go bye-bye?"

Preschoolers are notorious for asking, "Why?" because they are trying to understand and make sense of the world that they live in. In the midst of suffering, we ask the same question because we want to understand, in a logical sense, what is going on. When we can understand the world around us, when we believe that it is a predictable and logical place, we feel safe.

But the nature of suffering forces us to realize that the world is not predictable and not entirely logical, and not as safe as we would like to believe it is. And the question of God's goodness in the midst of it all can make all those Sunday school lessons we have heard seem insignificant.

Responses to the Problem of Suffering

In the 1800s and early 1900s, western European theology, largely under the influence of Friedrich Schleiermacher, taught that God simply wants us to be happy and successful, and that true religion depended on "feeling."

Then, in 1914, came World War I, with its trench warfare and the advent of poisonous gas. Nearly 20 million people died. Soon after came World War II with the unprecedented horrors of the Holocaust. Over 60 million people, nearly three percent of the world's population, were killed during World War II. Both wars were fought largely in western Europe. A whole continent, which had previously embraced an overly simplistic attitude about God, was forced to face the question of God's goodness in the midst of unspeakable suffering. Many people became agnostic or atheist.

When we find ourselves in moments of intense and often unexpected pain and suffering and are faced with the same question, we try to scramble for an answer to God's goodness in a world full of evil. And often our answers look like, "It's my fault. If only I had done this differently," or, "God must not be entirely good," or, "Maybe God just doesn't care." Some have even come to see God as sinister and sadistic, someone who takes a cruel delight in our pain.

The question of God's goodness and sovereignty in the midst of evil and suffering has been labeled by theologians "the problem of suffering" or "the problem of evil." Many theologians have attempted to answer the problem of suffering with less than satisfactory answers. One such answer is Deism, which says that God created the world but then stepped away from it; He does not interfere in human affairs. It is wrong to ask how God can be good in the face of suffering, because He does not involve Himself with what occurs on the earth.

Another proposed solution is Open Theism. Open Theism states that while God is all-knowing, this simply means that He knows everything that can be known. The future, however, is unknowable. If God knew the bad things that were going to happen to us in the future, He would surely intervene and prevent them from happening. God is entirely good, but because His knowledge is limited to the past and the present, He is unable to keep us from suffering.

Process theology, another potential solution, says that God is constantly evolving and growing, learning from His creation. He does the best that He can, but He is not powerful enough to curb evil.

While these different solutions may seem to provide nice and tidy answers to the problem of evil or suffering, they are in direct violation of what God reveals about Himself in the Bible. In response to the idea that rather than being Almighty, God is growing and evolving with His creation, Revelation 19:6 says, "Hallelujah! For the Lord our God, the Almighty, reigns." In opposition to the idea that God does not know the future, King David said, "Even before there is a word on my tongue, behold, O Lord, You know it all." (Psalms 139:4) And for the Deist, who believes that God does not care about the world, Hebrews 4:13 says, "And there is no creature hidden from His sight, but all things are open and laid bare to the eyes of Him with whom we have to do."

In saying that God is not entirely powerful, or that He is not entirely knowledgeable, that He would have helped us, He would have been there for us if only He were able, we are simply making excuses for Him. But in the Bible, He makes no excuses for Himself. On the contrary:

But our God is in the heavens; He does whatever He pleases (Psalms 115:3).

Remember the former things long past, for I am God, and there is no other; I am God, and there is no one like Me, declaring the end from the beginning, and from ancient times things which have not been done, saying, "My purpose will be established, and I will accomplish all My good pleasure" (Isaiah 46:9-10).

Furthermore, these "solutions" to the problem of evil and suffering still leave us looking for hope. And I am convinced that that is what we really want. More than answers, like Rachel, what we want to know is that our suffering will one day end.

Questions for Discussion/Reflection

You may want to answer these questions in your journal. If you are reading this book with a group, there may be some questions which you are uncomfortable answering, in part or in whole, with your group. That's okay! Be vulnerable to the extent that you are comfortable.

1. Do you think that it is important to understand the problem of suffering? Why or why not?

2. In what ways are you seeking an answer to the problem of suffering?

3. In regard to your own suffering, past or present, what is your typical response?

4. On a personal level, what does it mean to you that God's ways are higher than your ways and His thoughts are higher than your thoughts?

Chapter 2: Biblical Responses to the Problem of Suffering

Imagine that an average, run-of-the-mill Joe just landed a date with a superstar celebrity. He wants to learn as much as he can about her before their date—what kind of food she likes so he'll know where to take her to eat, what she's interested in, her style. He's standing in the checkout line at the grocery store and sees her picture on the cover of four magazines. He buys all the magazines, hoping to find some useful information.

When he gets home and opens the magazines, he finds that she dresses like a hobo, is a vegan, an avid supporter of PETA, and loves traveling to exotic places like Bangkok and Tahiti. This information scares him off a little bit; while Joe loves to travel, he also loves barbecues and has no problem swatting flies on a hot summer day. And he tries to look professional whenever he leaves the house. For a moment, he considers calling his date and cancelling, but he knows that his buddies would never let him hear the end of it.

After getting his pickup truck scrubbed and cleaned from the inside out and having his sister fuss over his outfit, he picks up his date from her exquisite Hollywood mansion. She looks nothing like a hobo; she is positively radiant. He asks her if she wants to go to an Indian restaurant, figuring that because of the Indians' disdain for meat, it would be a good choice. But at dinner, she talks about all of the fun that she had at last week's barbecue, and says that every chance she gets, she goes home to visit her family.

Joe is confused and says, "I thought you hated barbecues. Aren't you a vegan? I thought you spent all your free time traveling."

17

"Heavens, no!" she says. "Do you really believe what those silly tabloids say?"

How many false things are you believing about God that you heard from a source other than the Bible? Maybe you read something in a book or heard something from a well-meaning pastor or friend or family member. But just like Joe's date deserved the chance to tell him the truth about herself, God deserves our attention as He tells us the truth about Himself—the truth He has revealed in His Word. Let's stop reading the tabloids about God and look at what He has to say about His own goodness in the midst of evil and suffering instead.

Biblical Explanations for Evil and Suffering

There is a fundamental flaw in asking the question, "If God is good, why do bad things happen?" The flaw is that we are assuming that we understand God's goodness. But the book of Isaiah says, "'For My thoughts are not your thoughts, nor are your ways My ways,' declares the Lord. 'For as the heavens are higher than the earth, so are My ways higher than your ways and My thoughts than your thoughts'" (Isaiah 55:8-9). We have to approach the problem of suffering with the humility that says that we cannot understand the mind of God. Toward the end of the book of Job, after Job laid out all of his misery and doubts, God answered him by saying that He was so much greater than our understanding. Job responded humbly by saying, "I have declared that which I did not understand, things too wonderful for me, which I did not know" (Job 42:3).

This book is not simply about the question, "If God is good, why is there evil and suffering in the world, and why so much of it?" It is also about understanding God's goodness in the face of evil and suffering, and realizing that there is so much that we just cannot understand.

The Bible actually gives many causes for evil and for human suffering, and none of them necessarily contradict each other. Every explanation that the Bible gives provides for God's absolute goodness and sovereignty.

One explanation is the free will that God has given to people. God created us to worship Him and He wants us to worship Him freely, out of our own choice. He gave us the gift of free will so that we might come to love Him genuinely. But with that free will, we can also make bad choices, and in this fallen, sinful world that we live in, every single day people make wrong choices that hurt other people. All of us have been hurt by the sinful choices of others, and none of us is innocent of having hurt others. We have all hurt other people with our words, actions, and our lack thereof. We usually don't mean to hurt other people. But we still do.

Another answer that the Bible gives for suffering is that it is the judgment of a holy God on sin. The great flood of Genesis 6 and the destruction of Sodom and Gomorrah are both examples of God's judgment. But never assume that you, or anybody else, are suffering because God is punishing you for your sin. In the book of Job, his friends kept urging him to confess his sin so that God's judgment might cease and his suffering come to an end. Job insisted that his suffering was not due to his sin, and he was right.

"The first foster home that I lived at was one of the Roloff Homes that was closed down in 2000 for allegations of child abuse. The Roloff Homes were ultraconservative, and my housemother told me that God might kill my two brothers as a punishment for the sin in my life," said Nikki. But the God who reveals Himself in the Bible loves children, and He is not intent on punishing those who have been shattered. "A bruised reed He will not break" (Isaiah 42:3). When Jesus encountered a man who had been born blind, His disciples asked Him who sinned, the man or his parents, that he should be blind. Jesus answered that this was not the result of anybody's sin. It is very dangerous to assume that our suffering, or anybody else's, is God's judgment on sin. In taking this position we are setting ourselves up as judge when that position belongs solely to God.

The story of Job provides another answer for the problem of suffering. Job was not only one of the wealthiest but also one of the most righteous men alive, yet in one day he lost all of his children, servants, and wealth. Then he found himself covered with painful boils, and all he could do was sit in silence and use a piece of broken pottery to scrape his sores. What he did not know was that Satan had challenged God, saying that Job only worshiped Him because his life was so easy. Satan alleged that if everything was taken away from Job, he would curse God. So God gave Satan permission to take away everything except for Job's own life, in a test to see how faithful he really was. Sometimes our suffering is a test. But God does not ever test us so that we will fail. He tests us because He wants us to succeed, and He "who will not allow you to be tempted beyond what you are able, but with the temptation will provide the way of escape also, so that you will be able to endure it" (1 Corinthians 10:13).

Job's story illustrates yet another explanation that the Bible gives for suffering—that Satan and demonic forces are very real and very active. "Your adversary, the devil, prowls around like a roaring lion, seeking someone to devour" (1 Peter 5:8). I believe that there is a level of evil that cannot be attained even by human free will, but only by demonic influence. After the Holocaust, the modern world grappled with the question of how intelligent, world-class doctors could turn into the monsters who performed such infamous experiments on Jewish prisoners, killing them in droves. In Cambodia in the 1970s, Pol Pot imposed a policy of agrarian socialism, the implementation of which led to the death of two million people—twenty-five percent of his country's population. In one of his so-called "killing fields," there is a sign that reads:

We are hearing the grievous voice of the victims who were beaten by Pol Pot men with canes, bamboo stumps, or heads of hoes. Who were stabbed with knives or swords. We seem to be looking at the horrifying scenes and the panic-stricken faces of the people who were dying of starvation, forced labor or torture without mercy upon the skinny body.... How bitter they were when seeing their beloved children, wives, husbands, brothers, or sisters seized and tightly bound before being taken to mass grave! While they were waiting for their turn to come and share the same tragic lot.

The method of massacre which the clique of Pol Pot criminals was carried upon the innocent people of Kampuchea cannot be

20

described fully and clearly in words because the invention of this killing method was strangely cruel. So it is difficult for us to determine who they are for they have the human form but their hearts are demon's hearts.[2]

On January 12, 2010, an earthquake that registered 7.0 on the Richter magnitude scale struck the impoverished nation of Haiti and killed as many as 316,000 people. I was in college at the time; two weeks before I was due to give an hour-long presentation on the problem of suffering to my apologetics class, I was sent to Haiti as part of an emergency medical relief team. I will never forget seeing a dying man being carried to our tent in a wheelbarrow, nor what I felt when we had to turn him away because there was nothing we could do for him. The dead were piled in the streets; looking at all of the collapsed buildings, we knew that many more dead bodies were trapped inside and would not be recovered. A little boy kept coming to me and saying something in Creole; I later learned that he was asking for food. Every time an aftershock hit, pandemonium erupted because of the fear of more devastation. As far as I could tell, the Bible gave no explanation for this. We want to make sense of this world that we live in. We want to logically understand the things that happen to us. But sometimes, no matter how much searching we do, the answer remains elusive.

But there is another explanation for suffering, one that encompasses all of the above reasons, and ultimately provides the way out of suffering. That explanation is that the world that we live in does not ultimately follow the laws of logic; rather, it follows the laws of chaos. The next chapter is a brief introduction to chaos theory, and the rest of this book is about how chaos theory relates to suffering and to the kingdom of God.

Yes, God is good. And God is in control.

Questions for Discussion/Reflection

1. What are some things you are believing about God that don't necessarily come from the Bible? What are some of the "tabloids" about God?

---

2. Randy Alcorn, *If God Is Good* (Colorado Springs, CO: Multnomah Books, 2009), 132-133

2. What do you think it means that God's ways are higher than our ways? Do you think that we are able to understand His goodness? Why or why not?

3. Looking at the reasons that the Bible gives for evil and suffering, can you apply any of them to a situation (or situations) in your own life?

4. Can you think of any other biblical explanations for suffering or stories from the Bible in which suffering defies explanation?

Chapter 3: Chaos Theory

In the movie *Jurassic Park*, Ian Malcolm is a brilliant mathematician who specializes in a new field of study called chaos. When he arrives at the island where dinosaurs have been genetically engineered, he predicts that something small will soon cause the entire system to shut down catastrophically. Even though the park's computer system has been very intricately designed to account for any possible mishap, Malcolm insists that something can never be completely predicted. And the more complex a system is, the less predictable it is.

It doesn't take long for Malcolm to be proved correct. It is soon realized that even though all of the dinosaurs were engineered to be female, they are reproducing. Malcolm responds to everyone's perplexity by saying, "Life finds a way." Later in the movie he says, "If there is one thing the history of evolution has taught us it's that life will not be contained. Life breaks free, expands to new territory, and crashes through barriers, painfully, maybe even dangerously."

Malcolm's words may resonate with you. Sometimes life comes at you so fast that before you know what hit you, your whole world comes crashing down.

The Problem with Logic

Logic is a form of reasoning that essentially lays the foundation of traditional western thought. Simply put, it is something that just makes sense, so much that the same reasoning can be applied over and over again, in various circumstances, with the same results. For example, if you have a dog, I might logically conclude that you live in a house instead of an apartment. If you work in New York City, I might logically assume that you live there or at least nearby.

You are probably familiar with Isaac Newton as the man who discovered gravity. He was an astronomer, physicist, alchemist, philosopher, theologian, the list goes on. His work, *Principia Mathematica,* is considered one of the most important scientific books ever written. Some of the scientific laws that he discovered are that a body in motion tends to stay in motion, and a body at rest tends to stay at rest unless acted upon by an outside force. What comes up must come down. It's basic logic; this is how the world works. The world is like a complex machine with many parts, and all of the parts work together perfectly.

From the time of Newton, scientists have tried to understand the world in terms of cause and effect. If a seed has adequate soil, moisture, and sunlight, nine times out of ten, it will grow and develop into a plant. When I was in college, the easiest class that I took was meteorology. The second week of class, we did an experiment in which we "discovered" (as if we didn't already know it) that if you put ice into water, the ice will melt as the temperature of the water drops. I have a friend who loved algebra and calculus in high school, because she knew that she could always put the same numbers into an equation and every single time get the same answer. If you work the problem according to mathematical rules, which are always the same, you will always get the correct answer. In a sense, that was comforting. Logical cause and effect lets us know that the world in which we live is a safe and predictable place.

There is a degree of control that can be exercised over a logical system. If I leave a cake in the oven for too long, it will burn. If I don't want the cake to burn, I simply make sure that the oven's temperature is properly set and take it out of the oven on time. If I study what the teacher said to study and complete all of my assignments, I will do well in the class. If I do consistently well at work, I will get a raise or a promotion, right?

But life isn't always so simple. Have you ever followed a recipe exactly, only to find that dinner was a botched mess? I had a friend in college who was an extremely intelligent A student. But one semester she caught a bad case of the flu and had to miss over a month of school. Her professors were merciful in allowing her to make up the missed time, but there were some classes in which, no matter how much she studied, she simply could not catch up. She had to pay again for all of those classes and spend an extra semester repeating them.

The problem with logic is this—life is not logical. Life is chaotic.

The twentieth century saw a series of events that seemed to defy logical explanation—things such as World War I and World War II, the Great Depression, the Holocaust, the Armenian and Kurdish genocides. For many, the belief that the world is orderly and predictable came crashing down.

At the same time, some scientists were making new discoveries that defied Newtonian logic. Observing the odd behavior of electrons led to the development of quantum theory, which says things like *an object can be in two places at the same time*, and *an object's position and speed cannot be measured simultaneously.* In 1961, the meteorologist Edward Lorenz was using a computer to run a weather prediction. To save time, he used measurements which he had previously entered, but the computer had only saved the numbers to three decimal places instead of the six which he had originally entered. It seemed that the tiny difference in the decimal places should have been insignificant, but the result was an entirely different weather pattern. And thus began the formal scientific study of chaos.

Chaos is not some aberration of nature. While a logical view of the world is much more comfortable, what scientists are coming to find out more and more is that chaos is the natural order of things. Genesis 1:2 says, "The earth was formless and void." The original Hebrew word for "formless" literally means "a place of chaos."[3] The earth actually began in chaos.

The Butterfly Effect

A chaotic system is anything which shows extreme sensitivity to initial conditions. If something small, perhaps unnoticeable, is changed,

---

3. Brown, Driver, Briggs and Gesenius, "Hebrew Lexicon entry for Tohuw," The NAS Old Testament Hebrew Lexicon, http://www.biblestudytools.com/lexicons/hebrew/nas/tohuw.html (accessed January 27, 2014).

the entire system is affected. For example, if you add just a drop of dye to a large pitcher full of water, all of the water will be changed to the color of the dye. The effect of the dye, relative to the amount of water, is overwhelming.

On December 17, 2010, a poor Tunisian street vendor named Mohamed Bouazizi set himself on fire in front of the local police station to protest confiscation of his wares. Without his wares, he had no means to support himself and his family. By the time he died eighteen days later, thousands of Tunisians had taken up his cause. Protests and riots led to the downfall of the regime of the Tunisian President Zine El Abidine Ben Ali on January 14, 2011. Within days the revolution spread to Algeria, Egypt, Libya, Yemen, Iraq, Syria, Bahrain, Jordan, Saudi Arabia, and several other Arab countries. Protests in Cairo's Tahrir Square led to a virtual government shutdown, and a civil war erupted in Libya and Syria. I was living in Amman, the capital of Jordan, at the time. We were instructed to stay indoors on Friday afternoons because that was when protests usually occurred, and in the next few weeks some of them turned deadly.

I have to admit that I have never been very good at following instructions, and on several occasions my friend Kathleen and I ventured out during protests. On one such occasion, we found that the entire downtown area, which was usually packed to the brim with people, was eerily quiet except for some police barricades and a crowd of men standing solemnly in the street. At the noon call to prayer, they laid out their prayer mats in the street; and after praying, the protest began. As the mosques emptied, the crowd grew. There were several flags flying with a red hammer and sickle on them and the letters JCP, which I assumed stood for Jordanian Communist Party. I texted a friend on the other side of town to ask if she knew anything about that day's protest.

She immediately called me. "Are you downtown right now?" I could barely hear her above the din of the protesters.

"Yes," I said.

"Get out of there right now! This protest was organized by the Muslim Brotherhood and there are supposed to be as many as 100,000 people there. There have been reports that tear gas will be used!"

After taking a few pictures and videos we left, deciding that if an American was killed in an Arab Spring protest it might start another world war.

How could an unknown, impoverished street vendor spark a revolution that spanned the entire Arab world?

In June 1914 in Sarajevo, a 16-year-old Bosnian Serb named Gavrilo Princip shot and killed Archduke Franz Ferdinand of Austria and his wife, Sophie. What Princip could not have possibly known was that his bullet would begin World War I, in which nearly 20 million soldiers and civilians would be killed.

The butterfly effect is the term given to a relatively small change in initial conditions that causes a severe disruption. A small drop of dye placed into a large pitcher of water, the self-immolation of Mohammed Bouazizi, and the bullet that killed Ferdinand are all examples. All of these events were relatively small, but the outcome was unpredictably chaotic.

With the butterfly effect, the entire outcome can be traced back to a single event. The entire extinction of the dinosaurs can be traced back to a single meteorite. The fictional Ian Malcolm would probably go so far as to say that, according to chaos theory, a giant asteroid was bound to eventually come hurtling toward earth.

Feedback Loops

In the summer of 2007, the American housing market crashed. Not only were many homes sent into foreclosure, but hundreds of thousands of jobs in the housing sector—in construction, manufacturing, upholstery, etc.—were lost. With so many people out of work, the demand for welfare went up and consumer spending went down. As a result, many stores were closed and people who worked in retail positions found themselves out of work as well. More and more people were finding themselves in desperate financial need. Increasingly, more car loans went into default. With more people on welfare and food stamps and less tax revenue, the government had to make budget cuts in education, leading to more overcrowded classrooms and skyrocketing college tuition rates. This led to an increase in student loans, with some college graduates holding upward of $100,000 in debt. But with fewer jobs available, many have had to find minimum-wage jobs and default on their student loans. Everyone in America was hit by the recession.

This snowball effect is an example of a feedback loop. In a feedback loop, the consequences of an action result in increasingly greater consequences. X leads to more of Y, which leads to more of X, which leads to more of Y. And all the while, people caught up in this downward spiral find themselves asking, "Where is God in all of this?"

Questions for Discussion/Reflection

1. Do you tend to see the world as logical (making sense) or chaotic? Why?

2. How does this worldview affect how you see God?

3. How can your own suffering be described as chaotic?

4. When faced with the question, "Where is God in the midst of suffering?" what is/would be your response?

Chapter 4: What Went Wrong

Samuel was a young man growing up in a neighborhood called Alabama Village. With over a hundred murders a year, Alabama Village is the most dangerous neighborhood in the entire state. Like many other people in the Village, Samuel was extremely charismatic and showed much potential, but without a father or mother at home and the lack of positive role models, he made some rather poor choices. When he was 16, he shot and killed a man.

Samuel immediately turned himself in to the police and testified against the other men involved in the shooting. Because of his cooperation and his age, he was eligible to be tried as a juvenile, which would earn him a three-year prison sentence. Before the hearing which would determine if he would be tried with juvenile status, he was out on bond and smoked a joint of marijuana. At the hearing a week later, the judge was ready and willing to grant Samuel juvenile status, but first he had to take a drug test. Because he had smoked that one joint of marijuana, he had to be tried as an adult. Instead of getting three years in prison, he got twenty-five. The man Samuel shot just happened to be in the wrong place at the wrong time. He was dead and his family had to live the rest of their lives without him.

In the Garden

In the beginning, God created the heavens and the earth. He created all of the creatures of the deep—octopi, eels, whales, every kind of fish. He created everything that flies and everything that moves on the ground—birds, elephants, jaguars, zebras, lions, wolves, sheep. And then came the pinnacle of all creation, when God set His own likeness on the earth. One thing that amazes me is how Moses wrote Genesis 1.

A Theology of Chaos

If you are near a Bible, take a look at it. God said, "Let there be light," and there was light. God saw that it was good, there was evening and there was morning, and that was the first day. God said let there be an expanse between the waters, and God called the expanse sky. There was evening and there was morning, and that was the second day. God called for dry ground; there was evening and morning—the third day. God is creating the oceans, the mountains, the deserts, all of these beautiful things that we get to enjoy, yet Moses wrote it all in a way that is almost formulaic and doesn't necessarily invoke the imagination. Until God created man. And then Moses penned the first poem in the Bible:

> God created man in His own image, in the image of God He created him; male and female He created them (Genesis 1:27).

God set Adam and his wife in Eden, a veritable heaven on earth. That is the world that He created—a world without sickness, poverty, death, or sin. Everything that God made was good. But unfortunately, it did not stay that way for long, because evil incarnate, the Devil himself, entered the garden of Eden. In the form of a serpent, he approached Adam's wife, and led her to doubt God. "Indeed, has God said, 'You shall not eat from any tree of the garden'?" (Genesis 3:1).

"From the fruit of the trees of the garden we may eat; but from the fruit of the tree which is in the middle of the garden, God has said, 'You shall not eat from it or touch it, or you will die,'" was the woman's response (Genesis 3:2-3).

"You surely will not die! For God knows that in the day you eat from it your eyes will be opened, and you will be like God, knowing good and evil" (Genesis 3:4-5). But go back to Genesis 1:27. They were already like God! They were made in His image, and they were without sin. And they already knew right from wrong, because they knew that they should obey God's command to not eat from the tree in the middle of the garden.

When the woman ate the fruit and gave it to Adam, who also ate it, it was probably one of the most seemingly harmless events in all of history. Who would have ever imagined that eating a piece of fruit could have such disastrous consequences? Yet as soon as they ate it, they realized that they were naked and were filled with shame. When it was time for their afternoon walk with the Lord, He called out, "Where are you?" (Genesis 3:9). Not because He didn't know where they were, but because they didn't. When Adam and his wife confessed, what He said must have let them know that the implications of their action were huge. "What is this you have done?" (Genesis 3:13).

One generation later—not five or six, but after just one generation—their son, Cain, killed his brother, Abel. Can you imagine Adam and Eve's horror as they thought back to the garden of Eden and how their small act of disobedience led to their son's death? I imagine they would have given anything to be able to go back and erase the past. It wasn't long before things were so bad that God sent a flood to destroy humankind. Only Noah and his family were saved.

Paul describes in Romans how this one small event—disobeying God by eating a piece of fruit—changed everything. "Therefore, just as through one man sin entered into the world, and death through sin, and so death spread to all men, because all sinned" (Romans 5:12).

Many books have been written on God, evil, and suffering, and many different conclusions have been made about suffering and the character of God. But nobody has been able to explain the ultimate origin of evil.

We could go back to the garden of Eden and say that evil originated with Adam and Eve's sin. But without Satan, the very incarnation of evil, there to tempt them, they probably would not have eaten the forbidden fruit. We could go back further and say that evil began when the angel Lucifer decided that he wanted to become like God. But heaven is a place of absolute perfection, where all enjoy the presence of God. How could such an evil thought enter into Lucifer's mind?

A black hole is possibly the most chaotic object in the universe. Trying to understand evil is like looking into a massive black hole. One reason is that if you look at a black hole, you won't see anything. Not even light can escape from it. Another reason is that inside a black hole, all of the conventional laws of physics break down. Evil defies all of the laws that our natural minds understand, so that not even the most intelligent and biblically-sound theologian can explain the ultimate origin and nature of evil. Because all of the laws of physics break down inside of a black hole, scientists are forced to realize that there is much more to understand than the world that we can see. Evil forces us to realize that there is much more to understand, not only about the world, but also about the God who created it.

Everything that God made is good—even Lucifer. But somehow in this black hole of evil, Lucifer rebelled against God and became Satan. Adam and Eve, living in Paradise and in perfect communion with God, having absolutely no sin nature, disobeyed and ate the forbidden fruit. Where this black hole came from or under what laws it operates, I don't know. If you figure it out, please tell me.

As I explained in the previous chapter, the butterfly effect occurs when an *infinitesimally* small event creates an outcome that is completely beyond anything we could have imagined. This is what happened when Adam and his wife sinned. The perfect world that God created was set on a collision course with hell. The world is still a very beautiful place. All you need to do to realize that is watch a sunset. But in many ways, it no longer resembles the Paradise that God originally created.

The Butterfly Effect: Life Out of Control

Oftentimes we look at our suffering and try to understand it in a way that says that we could have prevented it. This is especially true for those who have suffered trauma and/or abuse. In a sense, it is comforting to feel that we had a degree of control over an out-of-control situation. As a result, many people blame themselves for the bad things that have happened to them, even things that were obviously not their fault. Victims of domestic abuse are notorious for trying to rationalize why their abuser attacked them, with reasons such as, "I didn't cook dinner right," or, "I opened my mouth when I knew I should have stayed quiet." This urge to blame ourselves is so strong that sometimes our brains actually rewire themselves so that we remember the event differently than how it actually happened. Instead, we remember it in a way that we feel as if we had control over the situation.

But the world that we live in is incredibly chaotic and more often than not completely out of our control. There was something that went wrong long before we were born, and it changed everything. Adam and his wife disobeyed God by eating the fruit from the Tree of the Knowledge of Good and Evil.

I am not trying to diminish the responsibility anybody may have had in another's suffering. I'm not trying to let people off the hook for what they did. All of the people who have hurt you are responsible for their actions, just like you are responsible for yours, and we will all one day stand before a just and holy God and give an account. But what I am saying is that to those of you who are, have been, or will be on the receiving end of suffering—which should be every person who has ever breathed—it was not your fault. Maybe if you had done something differently, it wouldn't have happened. But ultimately, you were born into a chaotic world, one that was already overrun with sin and suffering and out of your control.

What Was Lost

It is impossible to understate how much was lost from the fall. Stop and think about the worst thing that ever happened to you. Now imagine that it never happened. Imagine that all of the bad effects of that horrifying event are gone. Try to imagine a world without rape, without abuse, without drunk drivers, without war, without murder, without poverty. That is the world that we lost. "The fall, the first human tragedy, became the mother of all subsequent ones. We should do nothing to minimize it or pretend that it mattered less than it did."[4]

Take it a step further. Imagine a world with no natural disasters—no earthquakes, no hurricanes, no tornadoes, no tsunamis. "When Adam fell, earth fell on his coattails. The curse upon the earth is a curse upon Adam and his descendants."[5]

The bottom line is this: God created the world, and it was perfect. But through one small act of disobedience, sin entered the world and it has been wreaking havoc ever since. Today, thousands of years later, what we see is war, extreme poverty, social injustice, millions of orphans, genocide, and the list goes on. The deadly reign of sin will be discussed more in the next chapter.

4. Alcorn, *If God Is Good*, 57.
5. Ibid. 59.

Questions for Discussion/Reflection

1. What are some specific ways that the fall affects your life?

2. Can you recall a time when you were left saying, "If only"?

3. Have you ever tried to understand evil? What conclusion did you come to? How does that conclusion line up with the Bible?

4. Stop and think for a minute about the fact that you are created in the image of God. Does this change your perception of anything?

Chapter 5: Chaos and the Kingdom of Darkness

The idea of a kingdom is largely unfamiliar to the western world, which now consists almost exclusively of democracies and republics. Even the United Kingdom is not a true kingdom in the purest sense of the word; even though there is still a king and queen at Buckingham Palace, ever since the Magna Carta was signed almost a thousand years ago, the vast majority of power has been in the hands of Parliament and the Prime Minister. A kingdom is simply a land that is ruled by a king. The king may have a council of advisors and even a legislature, but ultimately most, if not all, of the authority rests solely with the king. Whether he is good or evil, competent or not, his word is law.

A good example of a true, if misguided, kingdom was Tsarist, or Imperial, Russia. Ivan the Terrible, who reigned during the 16th century, ruled all of Russia while seated on a ivory throne. However, he was mentally unstable and suffered bouts of severe paranoia and depression, which led to periods of violence in Russia during his rule. Regardless of his mental condition, Ivan had unlimited and undisputed power. Another example is the Roman Kingdom, which existed in ancient Rome prior to the Roman Republic and the Roman Empire. There was a Senate, but they served more as a council of advisors with little to no real authority. All authority essentially belonged to the king.

Satan's domain is actually a kingdom. Wherever he has authority, his decrees stand. And he has plenty of subjects—demons—who work to ensure that his authority remains intact. Satan does have authority—even Jesus acknowledged this when Satan tempted Him. When he said that he would give Jesus all the kingdoms of the world, Jesus did not deny that they were his to give. But as you will see throughout this book, Jesus ultimately took the keys of authority from Satan. Satan is a king and he has a kingdom, but the good news is, 1) you don't have to live in his kingdom, and 2) his days are numbered.

Satan's Authority

Jesus taught us to pray, "Your Kingdom come. Your will be done, on earth as it is in heaven" (Matthew 6:10). Why would He ask us to pray that the Father's will be done on earth? Because all too often the Father's will is not being done. Eliza's father left her and her mother shortly after she was born. Eliza always dreamed of her father riding in as her knight in shining armor, but as is all too typical with single mothers, Eliza and her mother lived in dire poverty. They were constantly in and out of homeless shelters. As a child, she was ashamed to do anything with her friends after school, for fear that they would discover that she and her mom lived in a shelter. A stepfather came into her life, taking the two of them out of homelessness, but also weighing her down with physical, verbal, and sexual abuse. This story is not a reflection of God's heart for His own precious creation. Rather, it shows how sin has distorted the perfect world that He created. God is not our enemy. He is not the author of evil and suffering. Satan is.

When Satan tempted Jesus, he promised to give Jesus all the kingdoms of the world if He would worship him. What is so astounding is that Jesus did not correct him by saying that the kingdoms of the world belonged to God. "Mankind's authority to rule was forfeited when Adam ate the forbidden fruit. Paul said, 'You are slaves to the one you obey.' In that one act, mankind became the slave and possession of the evil one. All that Adam owned, including the title deed to the planet with its corresponding position of rule, became part of the devil's spoil."[6]

Satan is called the prince of the power of the air, the ruler of this world, and the god of this world (see Ephesians 2:2; John 12:31; 2 Corinthians 4:4). Yes, he was defeated at the cross and through Jesus, we have victory over him. But in order to understand suffering from a biblical perspective, we must understand that we still live in a world that is very much ruled by the evil one.

6. Bill Johnson, *When Heaven Invades Earth*, (Shippensburg, PA, Destiny Image, 2003) 31.

Chaos and the Kingdom of Darkness

When Adam and his wife sinned by eating the forbidden fruit, God cursed the Devil, and also put a curse on humankind. The curse on the Devil is pretty extreme—for one, it says that women are going to be mad at him! But more importantly, the offspring of the woman, Jesus, would crush Satan's head, and Satan would strike His heel. God is essentially saying, "Satan, you are going to be destroyed. And women are going to have a role in your destruction."

In a nutshell, the curse on humankind was this—women will have pain in childbirth and desire for men, who will rule over them; the earth will produce thorns; men will work by the sweat of their brow (in other words, work will not be enjoyable); and ultimately, they will die. Every single day people experience the effects of this curse.

As we experience the curse, we multiply its ill effects. Have you ever said a careless word to someone and before you turned around that relationship was shattered? And then both of you carried that pain into your other relationships, so that they were harmed as well. As wounded people wound people, the effects of the curse continue to grow.

More often than not, the children who grow into adults who rob homes, murder, or become drug addicts or prostitutes are the children who grew up in unstable homes where they were unappreciated and oftentimes abused. King David is considered by many to have been the greatest king over Israel, but he had several wives and struggled with adultery. Solomon was his son through Bathsheba, with whom David had previously had an adulterous relationship. Like his father, Solomon also struggled with adultery; after years of ruling as the wisest king of Israel, his many wives led him to worship idols and false gods. One could actually say that it was Solomon's struggle with adultery that led to the division of Israel.

Is There Hope?

All of this seems pretty hopeless, but there is a promise hidden in the meaning of Eve's name. Until the curse is given, Eve is simply referred

37

to as "the woman," but in the verses following the curse, she is given the name Eve. *Eve* means "mother of all living." In the curse, God makes a promise of the offspring of woman, Jesus. Satan will bruise His heel, but Jesus will crush his head. Through Eve's descendant, Jesus, men will be set free from the reign of Satan and made alive.

Consider this: It was God, not Satan, who cursed humankind. At the end of the day, God, not Satan, is in control. If we are going to really take the Bible seriously, we have to believe that even through the curse, God is working all things together for our good. Nowhere does the Bible say that everything is good. But it says that God is working all things together for our good.

One way that God is using the curse for our good is that it teaches us, in very real ways, of our deep need for Him. Imagine that you are on an alien planet that is every bit as depraved as our own, yet not under the curse. An alien man punches his wife in the face, right there in the street, for no apparent reason. Then he turns on his kids. As you watch the scene with horror, you ask God to miraculously intervene. God responds by saying, "The people on this planet do not recognize their need for Me. Even though they are sinful, they see no need. They don't farm the land, yet it still produces plenty of food for them year after year. They are dead in their sins, and do not even realize it. They do not understand that this is not the abundant life that I created them to live. *But the wages of sin is still death, and they will still experience death as the ultimate curse of sin.*"

Living under the curse teaches us firsthand of our need for God. When Anne lost her son, after going through a period of rage against God for taking him, her response was, "Catch me, God, because here I come." Nothing else taught her of her need for God more than when she had to walk through her son's death. One reason God allows us to experience the consequences of sin is because it is at those times that we can truly appreciate our need for Him. Then we can be spared the ultimate curse of sin—spiritual death and an eternity in hell.

The curse on humankind allows us to recognize our need for God. And the curse on Satan, which is also a promise of the coming Messiah, provides a way out for us.

Questions for Discussion/Reflection

1. Why is it important to understand that Satan has a kingdom? How has the rule and reign of sin affected your life?

2. Do you know what your name means? How is the meaning of your name significant?

3. What do you think it would look like for heaven to come to earth? What would it look like for your family? For your city?

4. How has the Genesis 3 curse affected you? In what ways has it shown you your need for God?

Part 2: A Heavenly Perspective

Chapter 6: A New Perspective

Back in the early 1900s, there was a boy named Mark. He grew up in a small southern town, the kind where everybody knows everybody and their business, and every weekend fathers took their children to the river to swim. Except Mark's mother was unmarried when he was born, and he never met his father.

As a child, Mark watched with sadness as all of his friends did fun things with their dads. His best friend, Jerry, often invited him to go fishing with his dad. Over the years, Jerry's dad became like a surrogate father to him. He began to call him "Uncle Mike" and even honored him for Father's Day. Every Sunday, Uncle Mike took Mark and Jerry to church. Mark loved the extra time he got to spend with Uncle Mike.

One Sunday when he was twelve, there was a guest preacher at their church. He must have noticed that Mark and Jerry were sitting together with Uncle Mike during church because after the service, as he stood at the door to shake the congregants' hands as they left, he said to Mark, "Whose boy are you? You don't look anything like the fellows you were sitting with. Was your father sitting somewhere else?"

"Yes," Mark said, looking down. He justified his lie by telling himself that his father was somewhere else, and perhaps he was sitting down.

That afternoon, the three men grabbed their fishing poles and went out to the river. Uncle Mike noticed that Mark was unusually quiet that day. When he asked why, Mark told him what the guest preacher had said.

"Look at me," Uncle Mike said. "Look me straight in the eyes." After a minute, he said, "Ahh, yes, I see the resemblance. You look just like Jesus. You must belong to God." That day, his perspective on himself and the world around him completely changed.

That is what we really need—a new perspective. While it is true that he was fatherless, there was a greater reality that Uncle Mike had pointed out to him. Like Mark, we need to stop seeing only our present suffering. We need to learn to lift our heads and hearts upward to the One who is so much greater than anything else.

A Time for Everything

Solomon was King David's son and successor, and he filled those big shoes well. Solomon pleased God so much that God promised to give him anything that he wanted. Instead of fame and riches, Solomon asked for wisdom. God granted this request, and gave him fame and riches as well. Solomon wrote most of the book of Proverbs as well as all of Ecclesiastes, a sermon on how everything is futile except for the fear of God. In Ecclesiastes 3 is the well-known discourse on how everything has a time and a season.

To everything there is a season, A time for every purpose under heaven:

A time to be born, and a time to die;
A time to plant, and a time to pluck what is planted;
A time to kill, and a time to heal;
A time to break down, and a time to build up;
A time to weep, and a time to laugh;
A time to mourn, and a time to dance;
A time to cast away stones, and a time to gather stones;
A time to embrace, and a time to refrain from embracing;
A time to gain, and a time to lose;
A time to keep, and a time to throw away;
A time to tear, and a time to sew;
A time to keep silence, and a time to speak;
A time to love, and a time to hate;
A time of war, and a time of peace.

What profit has the worker from that in which he labors? I have seen the God-given task with which the sons of men are to be occupied. He has made everything beautiful in its time.

Also He has put eternity in their hearts, except that no one can find out the work that God does from beginning to end (Ecclesiastes 3:1-11 NKJV).

For a long time, this passage was very puzzling to me. I thought it meant that all of the things listed—birth, dancing, comfort, as well as killing, hating, and war—were all things that are necessary and ordained by God. There is a time when we have to give up, a time when we have to kill, a time when we have to tear down. It's as much a part of God's plan as loving our enemies and being peacemakers.

This led me to believe that all of our suffering is a part of God's plan for us and is caused, either directly or indirectly, by Him. The natural conclusion of this mindset, that God is the author of suffering, is that things like child abuse, rape, and starvation are necessary for Him to be glorified. We know that everything is working together to reveal the glory of God. Yet Jesus came with His message of loving your neighbor as you love yourself and His desire to bless children. If He really is the image of the invisible God, as the author of Hebrews said, then this is indeed a warped paradigm!

There are actually two different words for "time" used in this passage. Where it says, "There is a time for everything," the original Hebrew word used is *zaman* which refers to a set time.[7] Chronological time always has a set beginning and a set end. We might better read this verse as saying, "There is a set time for everything, a specific chronological period in which it will happen, and then it will come to an end."

But in saying, "a time to be born and a time to die," the word translated as "time" is the Hebrew word *'eth*.[8] This word means an experience or occurrence that happens, not chronological time. So the next verses are saying that mourning, throwing away, giving up—these things happen,

7. Brown, Driver, Briggs and Gesenius, "Hebrew Lexicon entry for Zaman," The NAS Old Testament Hebrew Lexicon, http://www.biblestudytools.com/lexicons/hebrew/nas/zaman.html (accessed January 27, 2014).
8. Brown, Driver, Briggs and Gesenius, "Hebrew Lexicon entry for 'eth," The NAS Old Testament Hebrew Lexicon, http://www.biblestudytools.com/lexicons/hebrew/nas/eth.html (accessed January 27, 2014).

as do healing and dancing and embracing. Look at what this passage says when the specific Hebrew meanings for "time" are substituted.

> There is a specific period of time for everything,
> and a season for every activity under heaven:
> the occurrence of birth, the occurrence of death
> the occurrence of planting and the occurrence of uprooting,
> the occurrence of killing and the occurrence of healing,
> the occurrence of tearing down and the occurrence of building,
> the occurrence of weeping and the occurrence of laughing,
> the occurrence of mourning and the occurrence of dancing,
> the occurrence of scattering stones and the occurrence of gathering them,
> the occurrence of embracing and the occurrence of refraining,
> the occurrence of searching and the occurrence of giving up,
> the occurrence of keeping and the occurrence of throwing away,
> the occurrence of tearing and the occurrence of mending,
> the occurrence of silence and the occurrence of speaking,
> the occurrence of love and the occurrence of hate,
> the occurrence of war and the occurrence of peace.

Even though Solomon was the wisest man who ever lived, he did not give an explanation for why these things happened. He just said that they do. We would do well to have Solomon's mindset and say that bad things happen, and it is not always clear why. But when bad things do happen, they occur within a set amount of time, and the season of suffering that we find ourselves in will come to an end.

Eternity in Our Hearts

Toward the end of the book of Job, Job learned a very important lesson about having a perspective larger than his present suffering. For most of the book he was questioning and blaming God for the terrible things that had been brought upon him. Then God speaks to him in the midst of his storm. And what is it that God tells him? Simply put, God tells Job that He is much greater than he can imagine. From this, Job gains a perspective that is much greater than his suffering. What he says from that new perspective seems like it is spoken by a completely different person: "Therefore I have declared that which I did not understand, things too wonderful for me, which I did not know. ...I have heard of You by the hearing of the ear; but now my eye sees You" (Job 42:3,5).

We are created in the image of God, and therefore hardwired with desires that reflect heaven. In every culture that I have been in, girls of all ages love to dress up and know that they are beautiful. Go tell a girl in your life, young or old, that she is beautiful and see if her eyes don't light up. Try to find a man who doesn't want to be around a beautiful woman. It doesn't happen. Beauty is one of heaven's greatest qualities. The descriptions of heaven in Revelation are absolutely breathtaking—a city of pure gold that is as clear as glass, gates made of pearl, the city's foundations made of precious stones (Revelation 21:18-21). Beauty is just one way that heaven's qualities are reflected in our desires.

Solomon put it perfectly in the verse following his talk on a time for everything: "He has made everything beautiful in its time. Also He has put eternity in their hearts, except that no one can find out the work that God does from beginning to end" (Ecclesiastes 3:11 NKJV). I think that what Solomon is really trying to tell us here is that we can have a different perspective. We can look outside of our present suffering, and while we cannot see the whole picture, we can see the God who really is working all things together for the good of those who love Him.

I think that what God wants to tell us in the midst of our own chaos is this: "What is happening to you is not beautiful. But you are."

Questions for Discussion/Reflection

1. Can you relate to Mark and his need for a perspective of a father? If so, how?

2. What do you think it means that God has set eternity in our hearts (Ecclesiastes 3:11)? On a practical level, what does it mean that He has set eternity in your heart?

3. What are some of heaven's qualities which are reflected in your desires?

4. What are some practical steps you can take to help change your perspective on suffering?

Chapter 7: A Biblical View of God in Suffering

The Black Death was without a doubt one of the greatest tragedies to ever strike humanity. It began in the Gobi Desert and spread to northeast China where it killed nine-tenths of the population during the 1300s; next it spread to Europe beginning in Italy via the trade routes. In a two-year period, one third of Europe's population died. It also spread throughout the Middle East during this same period and killed an untold number of people there. When the disease manifested itself in people, they became tired and developed a high fever. Next their lymph nodes swelled and turned black and they would begin to cough up blood; within a few days, maybe a week, the person was dead. Doctors could do nothing but watch their patients die, one after the other. Entire villages were wiped out. Fear of the disease was so great that parents would not take care of their sick children for fear of catching it. Many people were sure that this was the judgment of God, the end of the world.

The authority of the pope was temporarily cast aside as people tried to understand, in a personal way, why God had sent this horrible plague. When children died from the bubonic plague, a blanket cause was given, such as their failure to honor their parents, or because of their parents' sin. It was much like the ungodly response of Job's three friends. Public penance became such a common response that parades of people traveled from one village to the next, whipping themselves, hoping that God would forgive whatever sin had brought on the plague. Unfortunately, they were unknowingly spreading the disease from one village to the next, and opening themselves up to it through their self-inflicted open wounds. Whole villages of Jews were massacred by Christians because they thought that God was punishing the whole continent for the Jews' unbelief. Meanwhile, others were drinking in taverns—morning, noon, and night—figuring that they would soon die anyway. And all this time, the Black Death was killing both the pious and the ungodly indiscriminately.

While the brutality of the disease cannot be understated, the reaction to the Black Death in Europe was largely caused by an unbiblical view of God. During the Middle Ages, people were taught that they could buy God's forgiveness by giving money to various church building projects. During the crusades, hundreds of thousands of Jews and Muslims were massacred by European Christians who claimed that they were executing God's judgment. Our view of God has a profound effect on how we respond to suffering.

This story has another important lesson. The people stopped listening to the pope, and instead looked for answers directly from God. In the midst of suffering, it is natural to stop looking for the right theological answer and look for God instead.

In and out of our suffering, God's character is unchanging. Our perception of Him may change, but He does not. "Jesus Christ is the same yesterday and today and forever" (Hebrews 13:8). Suffering is like a cloud blocking the moon on a dark night, so that it is impossible to see God's true character. But through His Word and unchanging promises, we know that He is constant. He does not change.

Our perception of God is affected by many things. One of the most important factors in forming our perception of God's character is how we were treated by our earthly fathers. If your earthly father was around but emotionally unavailable, you probably see God as disinterested in your life, kind of like the statue of Abraham Lincoln. If your father was abusive, chances are you see God as a wrathful judge. If your father was good to you and enjoyed spending time with you, it is probably much easier for you to understand the Father-heart of God.

Other factors that affect our perception of God include hurts we have received, especially as children. Another big factor that affects us is our perception of the church; the way the church treats outsiders and "sinners" such as prostitutes, single moms, and homosexuals sends us a message about God. The recent sex abuse scandal by Catholic priests planted a seed of mistrust in the church and in God in people's minds. When Mary was 16, one of her classmates, Josh, was killed in a car accident after getting behind the wheel while drunk. She was in her high school's concert band and was asked to play "It Is Well with My Soul" at his funeral. Her father, who went to church every Sunday, objected because Josh was drunk when he died. That day she lost her last bit of respect for her dad because of his judgmentalism, but because of the way that members of her church loved her and let her know that she was special and appreciated, she did not give up on God. Things that can affect our relationship with God positively include positive experiences in the church, seeing answered prayers, and being loved unconditionally. Most importantly, the Bible, God's revelation of Himself, affects our perception of who He is.

We are not going to have a full or completely accurate view of God until we get to heaven, and then we'll have all of eternity to know Him more. But while on this earth, we can still have a view of Him that is solidly biblical. (The last chapter of this book is entirely about practical steps that we can take to finding God in the midst of suffering.) Many people think that it is impossible to know God's character. While living in Jordan, I was invited to a dinner party with several missionaries to the Middle East. I mentioned that knowing God's character has helped me to find much restoration in my life; one of the missionaries spent the next ten minutes berating me for thinking that I could know God's character. It is certainly true that much of His character is unknowable, because His ways are far above our ways and His thoughts are far above our thoughts. But He has chosen to reveal much of His character through His Word, and I have to believe that the reason He revealed it is because He wants us to know Him through it. Did He reveal His own self to us through the Bible so that we can make theological graphs and charts and come up with fancy Latin terms, but be ashamed to say that we know Him like we know our friends? Here are some of the attributes of His character that He has revealed to us.

Omnipotence

Omnipotence means "all-powerful." There is nothing that He cannot do. This doesn't mean something ridiculous like He can make a rock so heavy that even He can't lift it. It also doesn't mean that He can sin, because sin by definition means something that goes against His character. Omnipotence means that He can do anything that is in line with who He is.

Hezekiah was one of only three kings of Judah who feared God. Seven years before he ascended to the throne, Assyria captured the northern kingdom, Israel, and carried the Israelites off into exile. Twenty years later, the Assyrian army, under the leadership of the dreaded Sennacherib, entered the kingdom of Judah with the intent to destroy it. They overtook Judah's fortified cities and then laid siege to Jerusalem. Hezekiah had no recourse but to pray; isn't it amazing how so often prayer is our last resort—saved for when all of our resources have run out and our strength has failed? In one night, the Angel of the Lord came upon the Assyrian camp and killed 185,000 men. When morning came, there was nothing but dead bodies. Sennacherib returned to Ninevah, the capital of Assyria, and Jerusalem was spared (see Isaiah 36–39). Hezekiah's kingdom was not saved through military strength or a good strategy, but simply because God was on his side and fought for him.

Omnipresence

Omnipresence means that God is everywhere, all the time. Jeremiah prophesied, "'Am I a God who is near,' declares the Lord, 'and not a God far off? Can a man hide himself in hiding places so I do not see him?' declares the Lord. 'Do I not fill the heavens and the earth?' declares the Lord" (Jeremiah 23:23-24). David said, "Where can I go from Your Spirit? Or where can I flee from Your presence? If I ascend to heaven, You are there; if I make my bed in Sheol, behold, You are there. If I take the wings of the dawn, if I dwell in the remotest part of the sea, even there Your hand will lead me, and Your right hand will lay hold of me" (Psalms 139:7-10).

Have you ever felt like God has forgotten you? Many of David's psalms express that same feeling. "How long, O Lord? Will you forget me forever? How long will You hide Your face from me?" (Psalms 13:1). But God's omnipresence means that He is with you, all the time, even when you cannot see or feel Him. If He ceased to be with you, He would be denying His own self, and that is something that He simply cannot do.

Omniscience

Omniscience means that God knows everything. He doesn't simply know the past, He also knows the future choices that we will make and their consequences (see Psalms 139:4). He also knows how many hairs are on our heads. I don't know how many hairs are on my head or how I am going to respond the next time somebody is nasty toward me, so I think it is safe to say that God knows more about me than I do! The life of Deborah, Israel's only female judge, was marked by prophecy and victory. She was consistently victorious over Israel's enemies because of the clear words that she heard from God. God was able to tell her exactly what was to happen, every time, because He knew what was going to happen.

When Adam and Eve sinned by eating the forbidden fruit, they realized that they were naked and were ashamed before God. So they hid. God called out to them, "Where are you?" He didn't ask this because He didn't know where they were. He asked it because they didn't know where they were. Sometimes when I become painfully aware of my own sin, I want to hide from God by neglecting my quiet time and godly fellowship. But He still knows exactly where I am, because He knows my heart far better than I ever will.

Good

When Aimee was two, one of her favorite songs was a song about how big God is. One day she was singing it with her aunt, and could not understand for the life of her why it didn't also say how sweet God is.

"Aimee, there's not enough words to say all of the things that God is," her aunt said.

"Well, God is sweet," she insisted.

In the first chapter, I said that we cannot understand God's goodness. We cannot compare it to our own standard of goodness. While we can only see what has passed or what is happening right now, He sees the whole of history, the big picture, from beginning to end. Romans 8:28 says, "And we know that God causes all things to work together for good to those who love God, to those who are called according to His purpose." It does not say that all things are good. But God is good, and all things will ultimately work together for our good.

Agape Love

Agape is a Greek word that refers to sacrificial love. Perhaps the best real world example of sacrificial love is that of a mother. Your mother probably endured untold bouts of morning sickness and other ailments, then went through excruciating pain, all to bring you into the world. Just within the first five years of your life, how much did she sacrifice herself to meet your needs? But not everyone is fortunate enough to have a mother who loves them sacrificially. For those people, trying to understand *agape* love is a huge challenge. Isaiah 49:15-16 says, "Can a woman forget her nursing child and have no compassion on the son of her womb? Even these may forget, but I will not forget you. Behold, I have inscribed you on the palms of My hands."

The purest expression of *agape* was when Jesus died on the cross. The Son endured pain that defied all explanation. The pain of the whips and the nails was excruciating enough, but nothing can describe the pain of Judas' betrayal, Peter's denial, or when the Father turned His face away. And can you imagine the pain of the Father as He watched His beloved Son die? Truly greater love has no one than this—that a man lay down His life for His friends.

Humility

The idea of God being humble seems to go past all of our natural inclinations. But what could be more humble than God in heaven taking on human flesh and being born in a stable? Jesus said, "Come to Me, all who are weary and heavy-laden, and I will give you rest. Take My yoke upon you and learn from Me, for I am gentle and humble in heart, and you will find rest for your souls" (Matthew

11:28-29). Philippians 2:8 says, "Being found in appearance as a man, He humbled Himself by becoming obedient to the point of death, even death on a cross."

Holy

There is only one word which God repeatedly uses three times to describe Himself. The Bible never says that God is love, love, love. It never says that He is good, good, good or that He is humble, humble, humble. He is all these things and infinitely more. But the Bible says, over and over again, that He is holy, holy, holy. Every single thing that we can know about God has to be seen through the lens of His holiness. His love is holy. His goodness is holy. His humility is holy. His forgiveness is holy. His justice is holy. His mercy is holy. He is holy.

Isaiah had a rather dramatic experience when He was first called to be a prophet. He saw the temple of God and the angels encircling the throne of God, all crying, "Holy, holy, holy." His response was, "Woe is me, for I am ruined! Because I am a man of unclean lips, and I live among a people of unclean lips; for my eyes have seen the King, the Lord of hosts" (Isaiah 6:5). When Jesus appeared to the disciples while fishing, Peter said, "Go away from me Lord, for I am a sinful man!" (Luke 5:8).

Justice

In order for somebody to be considered for the duties of a judge, he must be able to clearly demonstrate justice. The role of a judge is to provide justice for both victims and criminals. If somebody stole a car and was brought before a judge, the expectation is that the judge will sentence him. If the judge refuses to sentence the criminal, his entire character will be questioned. For the person against whom the crime was committed, refusing to punish the criminal is like pouring salt on an open wound. God is a righteous judge, and when a sin is committed, that sin is committed against Himself.

Oftentimes when people think of the Old Testament, they think of things like the Great Flood, countless wars, and prophecies of doom. The image of God in the Old Testament seems to stand in stark contrast to Jesus, enough that some feel that the Old Testament is actually describing a different God! But we must understand that God is eternally just. And because of His justice, He must punish sin. The Bible is very clear that sin deserves death. "The wages of sin is death" (Romans 6:23). "Without shedding of blood there is no forgiveness" (Hebrews 9:22). Sin *must* be punished. That is why we see so many examples of wrath and vengeance in the Old Testament. It is God executing judgment on sin. We are seeing His justice.

Mercy

On one side of justice is judgment; on the other side is mercy. The wages of sin is still death, and that punishment must be paid; but God in His great and infinite mercy came to earth in the person of Jesus Christ. On the cross He paid the ultimate price of sin—death. God loves us so much that He allowed all our sin to be heaped on His Son, Jesus. On the cross God pronounced judgment on Jesus. Jesus paid the price for our sin. All who come to Him, believing in Him, do not have to face spiritual death—eternity in hell—for their sin because Jesus already died for it. God now looks on us with favor.

Forgiving

God is love, and we know that true love does not hold sins against others. Can you recall a time when somebody could just not let go of something wrong that you did? How about a time when you could not let go of something that somebody else did? That is not the nature of love. Love forgives. And through the death of Jesus, God's forgiving nature is revealed. He does not hold our sin against us, because He loves us. It has nothing to do with whether or not we deserve it. It has everything to do with His own character. We don't deserve our forgiveness, but He deserves to be able to forgive us.

Let's return to the idea that He can't do anything against His character; it is impossible for Him to not provide for you, because He is Jehovah-jireh, the Lord our provider. It is impossible for Him to not comfort you, because He is the Comforter. It is impossible for Him to not lead you in the path you should go, because He is the Good Shepherd. It is, however, possible for us to not receive what He has for us.

As C.S. Lewis said in *The Chronicles of Narnia*, He is not a tame lion. Understanding God is impossible. He is entirely unpredictable. Evil and suffering do not necessarily have a formula or direct cause, and neither does God's response. Who could have foreseen the cross as God's answer to evil?

Trying to understand God is not nearly as important as knowing Him. Not all of Jesus' miracles are fully understandable, such as when He healed a blind man by putting mud on his eyes. Why mud? Or when He healed the ear of one of the men who came to arrest Him. But every one of His miracles is an invitation to know God.

When we have a biblical view of God and truly know Him, it affects our response to evil and suffering. In regard to our own suffering, we have hope. We find deep within our hearts that He is not cruel, but rather that He is near to the brokenhearted. He is good, and because He is good, He is working all things together for our good.

In regard to the evil and suffering around us, it becomes impossible for us to stand there and wring our hands at the deteriorating state of the world. We begin to emulate His characteristics as we reach out to the poor and downtrodden. When Haiti was struck by the earthquake in January 2010, some pastors were busy saying that this was God's judgment on Haiti, but others were collecting money and relief supplies and sending people to Haiti in rescue teams.

Knowing God leaves no room for a hopeless view of the world. There's only room for Jesus.

Questions for Discussion/Reflection

1. What is the importance of having a biblical view of God?

2. What are some things that you can do to help you have a more biblical view of God?

3. What are some more attributes of God's character?

4. How does knowing God's character affect your perception of the world around you?

5. Name one aspect of God's character that you do not understand.

Chapter 8: Our Great High Priest

Many times people wonder why God doesn't do something about evil and suffering. But God did do something about evil and suffering. He became a man in the person of Jesus Christ. He experienced all our joys as well as our sorrows. And His death on the cross defeated the curse of sin and broke the authority of Satan. Jesus is God's answer to evil. Even when no one else understands, Jesus does. The Son of God became the Son of Man so that sons of men could become sons of God. And for those who have entered the kingdom of God and are living under the authority and kingship of Jesus, Satan is no longer the master. Jesus is. Nothing can get to you without going through Jesus first.

I said earlier that suffering is like a cloud blocking the moon on a dark night. It keeps us from seeing the light. But that does not mean that the light is not there.

The people who walk in darkness will see a great light; those who live in a dark land, the light will shine on them. You shall multiply the nation, You shall increase their gladness; they will be glad in Your presence As with the gladness of harvest, as men rejoice when they divide the spoil. For You shall break the yoke of their burden and the staff on their shoulders, the rod of their oppressor, as at the battle of Midian. For every boot of the booted warrior in the battle tumult, and cloak rolled in blood, will be for burning, fuel for the fire. For a child will be born to us, a son will be given to us; and the government will rest on His shoulders; and His name will be called Wonderful Counselor, Mighty God, Eternal Father, Prince of Peace. There will be no end to the increase of His government or of peace, on the throne of David and over his kingdom, to establish it and to uphold it with justice and righteousness from then on and forevermore. The zeal of the Lord of hosts will accomplish this (Isaiah 9:2-7).

Jesus as High Priest

The job of a priest is to serve as a mediator between God and man. One way priests would fulfill this function in the Old Testament was through making animal sacrifices, which covered the sins of the people. In the Old Testament, the ark of the covenant was in the central chamber of the tabernacle, in the Holy of Holies. The ark of the covenant was actually an altar, and an altar is the first and foremost place of sacrifice. It was the job of the High Priest to enter the Holy of Holies once a year and make a sacrifice over the mercy seat to cover the sins of the people.

Year after year, the high priest made a sacrifice over the mercy seat. But while the sacrifice *covered* the sins of the people, it is impossible for the blood of bulls and goats to *take sin away*. A massive curtain guarded the entryway to the Holy of Holies and symbolized the separation that still existed between man and God. When Jesus died, an earthquake caused that curtain to be ripped in two from the top down. Jesus became the great sacrifice that takes away the sin of all who believe, once and for all. And because of this, we no longer have to live separated from God. Like Adam and his wife before the fall, before the invasion of the kingdom of darkness, we can walk with God and have a relationship with Him. Through the sacrifice of His life on the cross, Jesus also became our great High Priest.

I was sitting with a friend who has two theological degrees, and we were discussing the role of Jesus as High Priest. What we came to is that we can discuss the theological significance of it all day, and that will prove to be very beautiful indeed. But on a personal level, what does it mean that Jesus is my High Priest? It means that we have someone who knows what life can be like and is able to relate to us in our need; He is not distant but close, and when we suffer He is right there with us. He already has an answer for us, and He is constantly interceding before the Father on our behalf. In short, as sons and daughters, we have inside access to the throne room of God. An old hymn, originally entitled "The Advocate" but now known as "Before the Throne of God Above," expresses His role as great High Priest beautifully.

Before the throne of God above,
I have a strong and perfect plea:
A great High Priest whose Name is Love,
Who ever lives and pleads for me.
My name is graven on His hand;
My name is written on His heart;
I know that while in heaven He stands,
No tongue can bid me thence depart.[9]

Jesus as Intercessor

Another role of priests is to intercede for the people before God. Because sin separates man from God, the priest serves as a kind of mediator between man and God. The prophet receives a word from heaven and brings it to earth, but the priest intercedes to heaven for the needs of the people. In other words, the priest is a prayer warrior. Psalms 99:6 says, "Moses and Aaron were among His priests, and Samuel was among those who called on His name; they called upon the Lord and He answered them."

Jesus fills this role of intercessor. The night before His crucifixion, Jesus did not only pray for Himself, He also prayed for us. Paul said, "Who is the one who condemns? Christ Jesus is He who died, yes, rather who was raised, who is at the right hand of God, who also intercedes for us" (Romans 8:34). Hebrews 7:25 says, "Therefore He is able also to save forever those who draw near to God through Him, since He always lives to make intercession for them." In the Old Testament, because of the priests' intercession and the sacrifices he made for the people, God would look with favor on His people. And because of Jesus' intercession and His sacrifice of His own life, God looks with favor on us.

---

9. Written by Charitie L. Bancroft, 1863, public domain.

Jesus Understands

While living in Jordan, I heard about a Sudanese family who emigrated to Britain after enduring the horrors of the Darfur genocide. At Christmastime they saw a nativity play at their church. Afterward, they told the pastor that the play was very good, but the most important part was left out. They told him that you haven't told the whole story of the birth of Jesus unless you include the part about all the baby boys being killed, because that describes the world into which He came.

In the midst of suffering, sometimes the greatest gift anybody can give us is being able to say, "I've been there, and I know what it's like." That is one of many gifts that God has given us in Jesus—somebody who understands. Hebrews 4:15 says, "For we do not have a high priest who cannot sympathize with our weaknesses, but One who has been tempted in all things as we are, yet without sin." Anything that we have suffered or will suffer, Jesus suffered to an even greater extent on the cross. Here is a list of some of the things that He suffered.

He suffered immense physical pain. He could have still accomplished the Father's perfect will without the thirty-nine lashes, the crown of thorns, or the nails piercing His wrists. But He chose the most painful death possible, and when relief for the pain was offered to Him, He declined it. Isaiah prophesied that by His stripes we are healed. By His wounds. His pain.

He was unjustly tried. All of us have experienced injustice at one time or another. Justice is so hardwired into our psyche that as children we often argue over who gets more than us. I remember countless arguments with my brothers over who got the biggest slice of cake or any number of things that seem silly to me now. Unfortunately, injustice is not always so petty. Right now Israeli jails are full of Palestinians who have been locked up for months, or even years, without even being charged.

Jesus' trial was incredibly unjust. The only witnesses brought forth could not even present concurring testimony. He was first accused of blasphemy, but according to Roman law this was only a minor offense.

He could not be put to death for blasphemy. He was then accused of inciting a rebellion. Pilate knew this was not true, but he permitted Jesus to be crucified anyway.

Jesus was betrayed and denied by His friends. Probably every person on this earth knows the pain caused by betrayal and denial. When it comes from one of your best friends, it is even worse. Judas and Peter had both walked with Jesus for three years. They heard His teachings, they personally witnessed His miracles, they were even given the authority to perform these miracles themselves. But at the darkest hour of Jesus' life, Judas betrayed Him for a few silver coins, and Peter denied that he ever knew Him. Out of the twelve disciples, John is the only one who is said to have been at the foot of the cross.

He was humiliated. Any victim of sexual abuse knows the true definition of shame and humiliation. So does Jesus. He hung naked on the cross.

He was rejected by His own people. Have you ever felt rejected by your family or those who should be supporting you? Jesus was a Jew, yet it was the Jews who wanted Him dead.

Jesus was abandoned, both by His disciples and His Father. "My God, My God, why have You forsaken Me?" has to be one of the most heartbreaking sentences in the whole Bible.

A girl named Lauren was struck to the core as she was struggling with the painful abandonment of her father. She felt like she was worthless and deserved to go to hell. One day she heard God say to her, "You're right. You deserve to go to hell. In fact, you deserve to be nailed to a cross and left to die. So that's what I'm going to do. I'm going to take all of the abuse, the shame, every beating you ever got, the rejection from your parents, and I'm going to nail it to a cross and leave it to die. The rape, the loneliness, the fear, I am going to turn my back on it. Look at this cross; look at every painful thing in your life hanging from it. I'm going to give it a name. I'm going to name it, Jesus."

All that Jesus has, He freely gives to us. He gave us His own life, taking on our sin so that He could give us His righteousness. He gives us peace. "Peace I leave with you; My peace I give to you" (John 14:27). He gives us favor with God. He gives us victory. And He gives us the Holy Spirit (see John 16:7). And the Holy Spirit is also interceding for us before the Father.

This means that God did do something about evil and suffering, and there is a way to be completely set free from the rule and reign of Satan. Because Jesus is our great High Priest, we have access to the Father and authority over the kingdom of darkness. Through Jesus you have authority over the Devil and have a place in a kingdom that is far superior to his.

Questions for Discussion/Reflection

1. Can you recall a time when you knew Jesus was praying for you?
2. Does knowing that Jesus sympathizes with you change your perspective on anything?
3. What does it mean to you personally that you have favor with God?
4. What else has He freely given you? And how can you walk in it?

Chapter 9: The Message of Jesus

When I was in high school, I visited my grandma's church in the backwoods of rural southern Mississippi. Little country churches are always a unique experience, especially when the Sunday morning service is cancelled because it's the first day of deer hunting season, or after church there's a big potluck and all the little old ladies make sweet potato pies and green bean casseroles and collard greens and banana pudding. This particular Sunday was right after Hurricane Katrina had devastated the Mississippi Gulf Coast. New Orleans got a lot of media attention because the levies broke and Lake Pontchartrain flooded, inundating the entire city with water. But the entire coast of both Mississippi and Alabama was also hit hard. People who worked offshore, either on oil rigs or on fishing boats, were out of work for months. Many homes, filled with lifetimes of memories, were destroyed. And many, many people died. The youth pastor stood in front of a group of teenagers full of questions about how the Lord gives and the Lord takes away. He held up his Bible and said, "This book is about a kingdom and a King."

The next few chapters are about the kingdom, which was the heart and soul of Jesus' message. But here, I want to focus on Jesus as the King. A kingdom is only as strong as its king, and without King Jesus, there is nothing left of the kingdom of God. One trap that I constantly fall into is seeking the benefits of being in the kingdom of God—such as God's provision in the most desperate of circumstances and finding the abundant life that He promised—but forgetting to sit at the feet of my King and remembering over and over again how much I love Him.

Therefore Pilate said to Him, "So You are a king?" Jesus answered, "You say correctly that I am a king. For this I have been born, and for this I have come into the world, to testify to the truth. Everyone who is of the truth hears My voice" (John 18:37).

The Authority of the King

One of the hallmarks of Jesus' ministry was His authority. Authority means that when you speak, people listen. It's like when the president of the United States walks into a room, and it becomes quiet because everyone knows that whatever he has to say, it is important and can impact a lot of people. Have you ever been in the presence of somebody who spoke and people listened? It doesn't matter how many degrees you have, how many letters come after your name, or what your job or position is if people don't listen to you. Without a voice that people will listen to, you cannot accomplish your task.

The Pharisees and Sadducees were like the Jewish political parties. They were responsible for making laws in the Sanhedrin, which was like their Congress. Most of the Sermon on the Mount is about the Mosaic law, in which the scribes and Pharisees were experts. After Jesus gave the Sermon on the Mount, the Bible says, "When Jesus had finished these words, the crowds were amazed at His teaching; for He was teaching them as one having authority, and not as their scribes" (Matthew 7:28-29). The scribes and Pharisees *were* the authority. But Jesus' authority was so much higher than theirs that it was as if they had none.

Authority also means that you are given a position of responsibility. Just before giving the Great Commission, Jesus told the disciples, "All authority has been given to Me in heaven and on earth" (Matthew 28:18). Jesus told a paralytic man who was brought to him for the healing of his body that his sins were forgiven. When the scribes and Pharisees accused Him of blasphemy, He said:

"Why are you thinking evil in your hearts? Which is easier, to say, 'Your sins are forgiven,' or to say, 'Get up, and walk'? But so that you may know that the Son of Man has authority on earth to forgive sins"—then He said to the paralytic, "Get up, pick up your bed and go home" (Matthew 9:4-6).

Not only did Jesus have the authority to teach, perform miracles, and cast out demons, He even had the authority to forgive sins.

Jesus' authority is important because a king must have authority to enforce his decrees. Good or bad, without authority a king's decrees are meaningless. But Jesus has authority, both in heaven and on earth. He even makes evil spirits listen to Him. Therefore, His decrees stand and will not ever pass away. Let's take a closer look at some of the decrees of King Jesus.

Healing

The message of Jesus is healing for those who live with brokenness from the kingdom of darkness. Jesus was fond of robbers (tax collectors) and prostitutes, even though He was often berated for it by the religious leaders. He said, "It is not those who are healthy who need a physician, but those who are sick; I did not come to call the righteous, but sinners" (Mark 2:17). Sinners—that's me and you. Sick people, both physically and spiritually, who need healing—that's me and you. His invitation is this: "Come to Me, all who are weary and heavy-laden, and I will give you rest" (Matthew 11:28).

Winston and some of his friends were praying for a man who had painful gout in his foot. When they were finished praying, he no longer had gout. George was allergic to shellfish for most of his life—until one day, he wasn't. God had healed him. It isn't only physical healing that Jesus has to offer. It's also healing from pain in the past and present and the daily struggles that can bring us to our knees by the end of the day.

Peace

The message of Jesus is peace. Seven hundred years before He was born, the prophet Isaiah prophesied that He would be called the Prince of Peace (see Isaiah 9:6). Micah, another Old Testament prophet, declared, "This One will be our peace" (Micah 5:5). At His birth, angels appeared in the sky, proclaiming, "On earth peace among men" (Luke

2:14). Jesus said, "Blessed are the peacemakers" (Matthew 5:9); "Peace I leave with you; My peace I give to you" (John 14:27). He even taught us to be peacemakers by saying things such as *love your neighbor as you love yourself*, and *love your enemies*.

In Matthew 10:34-36, He said, "Do not think that I came to bring peace on the earth; I did not come to bring peace, but a sword. For I came to set a man against his father, and a daughter against her mother, and a daughter-in-law against her mother-in-law; and a man's enemies will be the members of his household." The second part of this passage, in which Jesus said that people will be turned against each other, is actually a direct quote from Micah 7:6, a passage describing God's judgment on Israel. But the next verse, Micah 7:7, says, "But as for me, I will watch expectantly for the Lord; I will wait for the God of my salvation. My God will hear me." In this instance, Jesus quoted an Old Testament passage about God's judgment because soon God's judgment would be executed. First, God's judgment on our sins was placed on Jesus when He died on the cross. And when Israel rejected its Messiah, God's judgment was executed a second time—this time on them. In the year AD 70, the Romans destroyed Jerusalem, including the temple. If God's judgment was placed on Jesus instead of you, then there is nothing left for you but peace.

No Condemnation

John 3:16 is easily the most famous verse of all time. It summarizes the entire gospel in just a few short lines. The next one, though, is just as important, because it derails many of our anxieties about Jesus. John 3:17 says that Jesus did not come to condemn us. He came to save us.

The Old Testament is filled with images of God's wrath on sinful man. So how is it possible that God's own Son would bring a message that is so different, and at times actually seems to be entirely contradictory to the rest of the Bible? It's because before Jesus, the whole world was condemned. Their sins had separated them from a just and holy God. Without Jesus, you and I stand condemned. Jesus did not need to bring a message of condemnation because we were already condemned. The message of Jesus is all about the kingdom of God coming down to earth and a new covenant coming with it.

Half of Jesus' message is summed up in Matthew 11:28: "Come to Me, all who are weary and heavy-laden, and I will give you rest." The other half is found in Matthew 28:18-20:

> And Jesus came up and spoke to them, saying, "All authority has been given to Me in heaven and on earth. Go therefore and make disciples of all the nations, baptizing them in the name of the Father and the Son and the Holy Spirit, teaching them to observe all that I commanded you; and lo, I am with you always, even to the end of the age."

Questions for Discussion/Reflection

1. What does it mean that the Bible is about a kingdom and a King? Why is it important to understand that—both in and out of suffering?

2. On a personal level, what does it mean that Jesus has authority?

3. Have you ever wondered if miraculous healings still occur? How has that affected your perception of Jesus?

4. Have you ever felt condemned by the church? How has that affected your perception of God? What does it mean that Jesus did not come to condemn?

Part 3: Kingdom Chaos

Chapter 10: The Unstoppable Kingdom

The term *butterfly effect*, the idea that small changes in initial conditions can drastically change a situation's outcome, was coined by Edward Lorenz, the meteorologist who accidentally discovered chaos. It was initially used to describe unpredictable changes in the weather, with the theoretical notion that whether or not a hurricane developed might depend on something infinitesimally small, such as whether or not a butterfly had flapped its wings a few days before. Weather is, in fact, a chaotic system. That is why it cannot be predicted more than a few days in advance, and oftentimes those predictions are wrong. Hurricanes are especially chaotic. I grew up on the Gulf Coast, and several times my city was put under an evacuation warning because a hurricane was expected to make landfall within the next day or two.

Shortly after Hurricane Katrina destroyed New Orleans and the Mississippi and Alabama coasts, Hurricane Rita came into the gulf and was set to make landfall over Victoria, Texas, where I lived at the time, as a Category 5 storm. Schools and offices were closed and everybody was ordered to evacuate. After the town was essentially deserted, Rita changed paths and struck the Texas/Louisiana border as a Category 3. We returned home to find a few rain puddles and blown leaves. Hurricanes are impossible to predict because they are chaotic.

Likewise, in the Sea of Galilee unpredicatable, chaotic storms appear from seemingly nowhere. But as chaotic as the things that we face in life are—like unpredictable storms in both the weather and our own lives—they are subject to the rule and reign of God through Jesus.

On that day, when evening came, He said to them, "Let us go over to the other side." Leaving the crowd, they took Him along with them in the boat, just as He was; and other boats were with Him. And there arose a fierce gale of wind, and the waves were breaking over the boat so much that the boat was already filling up. Jesus Himself was in the stern, asleep on the cushion; and they woke Him and said to Him, "Teacher, do You not care that we are perishing?" And He got up and rebuked the wind and said to the sea, "Hush, be still." And the wind died down and it became perfectly calm. And He said to them, "Why are you afraid? Do you still have no faith?" They became very much afraid and said to one another, "Who then is this, that even the wind and the sea obey Him?" (Mark 4:35-41)

The End of Satan's Authority

Daniel 7:1-6 tells of three great and terrifying beasts that came out of the sea. They were given authority to devour and rule. Then a fourth beast comes:

After this I kept looking in the night visions, and behold, a fourth beast, dreadful and terrifying and extremely strong; and it had large iron teeth. It devoured and crushed and trampled down the remainder with its feet; and it was different from all the beasts that were before it, and it had ten horns. While I was contemplating the horns, behold, another horn, a little one, came up among them, and three of the first horns were pulled out by the roots before it; and behold, this horn possessed eyes like the eyes of a man and a mouth uttering great boasts (Daniel 7:7-8).

While the fourth beast is symbolic of an earthly kingdom, it also refers to Satan and his rule. Satan knows that he has a kingdom and that he is the prince of the power of the air. He knows that he has authority on this earth. The sin that originally got Lucifer expelled from heaven was that he wanted to be like God, and in this vision he speaks boastfully against God again. He is a bit of a hothead.

But there is a point in actual history in which the court is seated, the books are opened, and judgment is passed on Satan.

I kept looking until thrones were set up, and the Ancient of Days took His seat; His vesture was like white snow and the hair of His head like pure wool. His throne was ablaze with flames, its wheels were a burning fire. A river of fire was flowing and coming out from before Him; thousands upon thousands were attending Him, and myriads upon myriads were standing before Him; the court sat, and the books were opened.

Then I kept looking because of the sound of the boastful words which the horn was speaking; I kept looking until the beast was slain, and its body was destroyed and given to the burning fire. As for the rest of the beasts, their dominion was taken away, but an extension of life was granted to them for an appointed period of time.

I kept looking in the night visions, and behold, with the clouds of heaven one like a Son of Man was coming, and He came up to the Ancient of Days and was presented before Him. And to Him was given dominion, glory and a kingdom, that all the peoples, nations and men of every language might serve Him. His dominion is an everlasting dominion which will not pass away; and His kingdom is one which will not be destroyed (Daniel 7:9-14).

The interpretation of the vision, found in the next few verses, tells us that the beasts will wage war against the saints, and for a time the saints will be losing to the beasts. They will be overpowered. But the Ancient of Days, God Himself, will come and pronounce judgment in favor of the saints, and they will be given a kingdom that can never be destroyed.

But the court will sit for judgment, and his dominion will be taken away, annihilated and destroyed forever. Then the sovereignty, the dominion and the greatness of all the kingdoms under the whole heaven will be given to the people of the saints of the Highest One; His kingdom will be an everlasting kingdom, and all the dominions will serve and obey Him (Daniel 7:26-27).

A Theology of Chaos

There was a time when Satan overwhelmed even the saints of the Most High God. But the night before His death, Jesus said that the prince of this world now stands condemned (see John 16:11). At the cross, Satan's authority was taken away and judgment was pronounced in favor of the saints. In favor of us. And because of Jesus, we are given a kingdom that is far superior to Satan's. The kingdom is *given* to us, for us to possess. And this kingdom, the kingdom of God, is God's perfect solution to man's deepest need. Satan's kingdom has left all of us ravaged and beaten. But the kingdom of God is far superior to Satan's. "In the world you have tribulation, but take courage; I have overcome the world" (John 16:33).

What the Kingdom Stands For

The kingdom of God changes everything. Here are some examples of what the kingdom can do for a person. I include some Old Testament verses, because Old Testament promises point to the kingdom.

Comfort for Those who Mourn
Blessed are *those who mourn*, for they *shall be comforted* (Matthew 5:4).

Satisfaction for the Hungry
Blessed are *those who hunger* and thirst for righteousness, for they *shall be satisfied* (Matthew 5:6).

Adoption for the Orphan
He predestined us to *adoption as sons* through Jesus Christ to Himself, according to the kind intention of His will (Ephesians 1:5).

Honor for the Servant
If anyone serves Me, he must follow Me; and where I am, there My servant will be also; if anyone serves Me, *the Father will honor him* (John 12:26).

Freedom for the Captives, Peace for the Brokenhearted, Justice for the Oppressed, and Beauty for Ashes
The Spirit of the Lord God is upon me, because the Lord has anointed me to bring good news to the afflicted; He has sent me to *bind up the brokenhearted*, to proclaim *liberty to captives and freedom to*

prisoners; to proclaim the favorable year of the Lord and the day of *vengeance of our God*; to comfort all who mourn, to grant those who mourn in Zion, giving them a *garland instead of ashes*, the oil of gladness instead of mourning, the mantle of praise instead of a spirit of fainting. So they will be called oaks of righteousness, the planting of the Lord, that He may be glorified (Isaiah 61:1-3).

Favor for the Sinner
Glory to God in the highest, and on earth *peace among men with whom He is pleased* (Luke 2:14).

Joy for the Grieving
Truly, truly, I say to you, that you will weep and lament, but the world will rejoice; you will grieve, but *your grief will be turned into joy* (John 16:20).

Grace for the Broken
My grace is sufficient for you, for power is perfected in weakness (2 Corinthians 12:9).

Healing for the Sick
And hearing this, Jesus said to them, "It is not those who are healthy who need a physician, but *those who are sick; I did not come to call the righteous, but sinners*" (Mark 2:17).

Rest for the Weary
Come to Me, all who are weary and heavy-laden, and I will give you *rest* (Matthew 11:28).

Hope for the Seeking
You will *seek Me and find Me* when you search for Me with all your heart (Jeremiah 29:13).

Purpose for the Restless
But, indeed, *for this reason I have allowed you to remain*, in order to show you My power and in order to proclaim My name through all the earth (Exodus 9:16).

For the Scripture says to Pharaoh, *"For this very purpose I raised you up*, to demonstrate My power in you, and that My name might be proclaimed throughout the whole earth" (Romans 9:17).

Rescue for the Wanderer
What do you think? If any man has a hundred sheep, and one of them has gone astray, does he not leave the ninety-nine on the mountains and *go and search for the one that is straying*? If it turns out that he finds it, truly I say to you, he rejoices over it more than over the ninety-nine which have not gone astray. So it is not the will of your Father who is in heaven that one of these little ones perish (Matthew 18:12-14).

Prosperity for the Poor
Every one who thirsts, come to the waters; and you who have no money come, buy and eat. Come, buy wine and milk without money and without cost. Why do you spend money for what is not bread, and your wages for what does not satisfy? Listen carefully to Me, and eat what is good, and *delight yourself in abundance* (Isaiah 55:1-2).

Comfort for the Humble
"I have seen his ways, but I will heal him; I will lead him and *restore comfort to him* and to his mourners, creating the praise of the lips. Peace, peace to him who is far and to him who is near," says the Lord, "and I will heal him" (Isaiah 57:18-19).

Forgiveness for the Sinner
For this reason I say to you, her sins, which are many, *have been forgiven*, for she loved much; but he who is forgiven little, loves little (Luke 7:47).

Compassion for the Forgotten
Can a woman forget her nursing child and have no compassion on the son of her womb? Even these may forget, but *I will not forget you*. Behold, I have inscribed you on the palms of My hands; your walls are continually before Me (Isaiah 49:15-16).

Redemption for the Abandoned

"For your husband is your Maker, whose name is the Lord of hosts; and your Redeemer is the Holy One of Israel, who is called the God of all the earth. For *the Lord has called you*, like a wife forsaken and grieved in spirit, even like a wife of one's youth when she is rejected," says your God (Isaiah 54:5-6).

Defense for the Widow and Orphan

A *father of the fatherless and a judge for the widows*, is God in His holy habitation (Psalms 68:5).

Sight for the Blind, Healing for the Lame, Hearing for the Deaf, New Life for the Dead, and Cleansing for the Leper

The *blind receive sight* and the *lame walk*, the *lepers are cleansed and the deaf hear*, the *dead are raised up*, and the *poor have the gospel* preached to them (Matthew 11:5).

Unconditional Love for All

"For the mountains may be removed and the hills may shake, but *My lovingkindness will not be removed from you*, and My covenant of peace will not be shaken," says the Lord who has compassion on you (Isaiah 54:10).

Now that is good news!

The Kingdom in the New Testament

The message of the kingdom in the New Testament begins with John the Baptist, who proclaimed that the kingdom of heaven was near. Jesus began His ministry by saying, "The time is fulfilled, and the kingdom of God is at hand; repent and believe in the gospel" (Mark 1:15).

The Sermon on the Mount, considered the greatest sermon ever written, begins with, "Blessed are the poor in spirit, for theirs is the kingdom of heaven" (Matthew 5:3). It ends with the parable of the man who built his house upon the rock, the rock symbolizing the kingdom (see Matthew 7:21-27). When His disciples asked Him to teach them to pray, He taught them to pray for the coming of the kingdom (see Luke 11:1-2). The message of the kingdom was so crucial to everything that Jesus taught that He actually calls His message the *good news of the kingdom* (see Matthew 24:14).

After Jesus came back to life, we see that all through His ministry His disciples had been thinking that He was going to restore the kingdom to Israel (see Acts 1:6). Jesus changed the subject and said, "You will receive power when the Holy Spirit has come upon you; and you shall be My witnesses both in Jerusalem, and in all Judea and Samaria, and even to the remotest part of the earth" (Acts 1:8). It's as if Jesus was saying, "The kingdom is already here! I am the One who reigns on David's throne. And you are My ambassadors who will proclaim the message of the kingdom far beyond the borders of Israel."

Questions for Discussion/Reflection

1. What does it mean that the kingdom has been given to you, as prophesied in the Daniel passage?

2. God has pronounced judgment in your favor, but His judgment is against Satan. Why is that significant?

3. In the list of things that the kingdom stands for, which one stood out the most to you? Why?

4. Why is it important that the kingdom of God is not an earthly kingdom, as the disciples had hoped?

Chapter 11: Chaos and the Kingdom

Have you ever noticed how much imagery from nature is used in the Bible? As a theology student, I often had to analyze the symbolism of things such as mountains, clouds, and water. But for all of my work, and even though I had A's, I never really learned anything new about God. I could chart and graph and analyze all of the symbolism, but nothing compares to actually standing on the shore of the ocean, or climbing a mountain out in the middle of the desert. Then you can't help but understand what the biblical authors meant when they said things such as, "Our God is a consuming fire" (Hebrews 12:29), or, "But let justice roll down like waters and righteousness like an ever-flowing stream" (Amos 5:24). The world is His. Satan may have authority in this world, but God has authority over Satan. Ultimately, this world *is* God's. Just as the work of the artist is a reflection of the artist himself, so nature reveals much about the God who created it.

Before the mid-1900s, mathematics was only able to explain the things that man could create, such as buildings, roads, or the ancient pyramids. It could explain straight lines, circles, curves, etc., but math and nature were like two magnetic north poles that repelled each other. But in the mid-1900s, a mathematician named Benoit Mandelbrot looked at the patterns found in nature and noticed striking similarities. Rather than being random forms and conglomerations, he discovered something he called self-similarity. For example, if you look at a large cloud, you will notice a unique design that repeats itself to form the overall shape of the cloud. Look at a smaller patch of the cloud, and you will notice the same design but on a smaller scale. Look at an even smaller patch of the cloud, and you will see the same thing. The same holds true for the shape of a mountain, the veins of a leaf, or the contours on a shell. Images of the bands on Jupiter and even the pulses of stars show the same repeating patterns. Look closely in a mirror at the iris of your own eye. All of creation exhibits these repeating patterns, which are called fractals.

Mandelbrot was able to look at nature and mathematics in a new and revolutionary way. The mathematical equations he discovered created brilliant, extraordinary images that bear no resemblance at all to the lines and parabolas you probably had to graph in high school and college. Fractals and fractal equations describe the natural world that God created, and they are a crucial aspect of chaos mathematics. What can this mean except that nature is extremely chaotic? When this is combined with the natural imagery used throughout the Bible, the other medium through which the Great Artist expresses Himself, the only conclusion I can draw is that the kingdom of God is chaotic as well.

Kingdom Growth

Jesus uses several parables to demonstrate the growth of the kingdom. The first of these is the parable of the four soils, told in Matthew 13:3-23. A farmer went out to sow some seeds. Some seed fell along the path, and the birds ate it. Some fell on rocky soil. The plants sprang up quickly, but because they had no roots, as soon as the sun came out it scorched them. Some fell among thorns, which choked out the plants. But some of it fell on good soil and produced a crop, *up to a hundred times what was sown*. A small seed grows into a plant, which produces many more seeds. That kind of growth is chaotic.

The kingdom cannot come from nothing. It can come into and forever change a person who has nothing, but it has to begin with something—with a seed and good soil. The unseen hero in this story is the plower who spent countless hours and days preparing the good soil. Who are some of the people in your life who helped prepare you for the message of the kingdom? The seed is the message of the kingdom, and the soil is your heart. Take a minute and close your eyes and imagine that a seed of your favorite kind of fruit has been planted in your heart. It grows into a tree or a vine or whatever; after you have eaten all that you can handle, you just give it all away to everyone around you. Now everyone around you has tasted and seen that the Lord is good. In addition, they also have the seed of the kingdom because it was in the fruit that you gave them. What else is happening? As hearts are taken captive by the kingdom of God, the kingdom of darkness is losing dominion.

In this parable, Jesus demonstrates how the growth of the kingdom reproduces exponentially. Earlier I talked about how the kingdom of darkness reproduces itself—wounded people wound people, and so the chaos caused by sin's devastation spreads. But the reproductive growth of the kingdom of God is described as a plant. A plant is alive. A plant bears fruit that can be eaten. And a plant produces seeds, which become entirely new plants. The kingdom of God is alive and it brings life, even more rapidly than the kingdom of darkness destroys.

Jesus tells two more parables about kingdom growth in Matthew 13:31-33. The first is about a mustard seed, a tiny seed that grows into a giant tree. Anybody who has ever seen a mustard plant knows that here Jesus is using hyperbole. Mustard plants are relatively small, but the point is still that the growth of the seed is incredibly dramatic. The seeds are very small, but within just a few months a dormant seed can become a flourishing plant that can be used for food and reproduces many more seeds. This describes how quickly the kingdom grows and changes people. Once the seed grows into a plant, it can never again be a seed. But it can produce hundreds of new seeds, each of which has the potential to grow into a brand-new plant.

The second parable is about yeast—how a tiny bit of yeast works through an entire batch of dough. While in the Bible yeast is typically analogous to sin, especially the sin of pride, here it describes the chaotic movement of the kingdom. If you have ever made bread, you know what I am talking about. Give a batch of dough a tiny bit of yeast and let it sit for an hour, and the dough will easily double in size. Here Jesus is essentially describing the butterfly effect! The dough cannot return to its original state, ever. But you can save a piece of that dough, and it will be enough to change a whole other batch of dough.

Kingdom growth is both irreversible and reproductive. The kingdom causes people to be permanently changed, and it does it in such a way that they can't help but bring the kingdom to those around them.

The Butterfly Effect

Let's take a look at the death of Jesus from the perspective of 2,000 years ago. The Romans executed many people. Anyone who got in their way was immediately killed—criminals, insurrectionists, would-be kings, anybody. These are the people who watched gladiators fight to the death for entertainment! The execution of a Jewish itinerant preacher in the backwater of the empire was seemingly of no consequence—except that when He died, the curtain that guarded the entrance to the Holy of Holies was ripped in two.

Remember how the kingdom of darkness began with a tiny event? Adam and Eve disobeyed God by eating a piece of fruit. Something so insignificant and small brought about the chaotic rule of Satan. In Romans, Paul compared Jesus' death to Adam's sin.

Therefore, just as through one man sin entered into the world, and death through sin, and so death spread to all men, because all sinned—for until the Law sin was in the world, but sin is not imputed when there is no law. Nevertheless death reigned from Adam until Moses, even over those who had not sinned in the likeness of the offense of Adam, who is a type of Him who was to come.

But the free gift is not like the transgression. For if by the transgression of the one the many died, much more did the grace of God and the gift by the grace of the one Man, Jesus Christ, abound to the many. The gift is not like that which came through the one who sinned; for on the one hand the judgment arose from one transgression resulting in condemnation, but on the other hand the free gift arose from many transgressions resulting in justification. For if by the transgression of the one, death reigned through the one, much more those who receive the abundance of grace and of the gift of righteousness will reign in life through the One, Jesus Christ.

So then as through one transgression there resulted condemnation to all men, even so through one act of righteousness there resulted justification of life to all men. *For as through the one man's disobedience the many were made sinners, even so through the obedience of the One the many will be made righteous* (Romans 5:12-19).

The crucifixion and resurrection of Jesus was like a small blip in the record of human history. But that small blip changed everything. It brought the kingdom of God down to earth and began its expansion. It has been expanding for the past 2,000 years, overthrowing the powers of darkness that have held humankind in bondage.

The Uncontrollable Kingdom

Jesus said a lot about how our faith can do powerful things. "If you have faith the size of a mustard seed, you will say to this mountain, 'Move from here to there,' and it will move; and nothing will be impossible to you" (Matthew 17:20). "Truly, truly, I say to you, he who believes in Me, the works that I do, he will do also; and greater works than these he will do; because I go to the Father. Whatever you ask in My name, that will I do, so that the Father may be glorified in the Son. If you ask Me anything in My name, I will do it" (John 14:12-14).

I know that what Jesus said here is true. Not only because He said it, but also because I have seen it in my own life and in the lives of many close friends. But for a long time I thought that if I believed something hard enough and had enough faith, God would make it happen. When I was eleven, one of my closest friends moved to a different state. We had been absolutely best friends; we had cried on each others' shoulders and everything. When she left I was devastated. And somehow in my eleven- and twelve-year-old mind, I got the idea that if I believed hard enough, I could somehow teleport from Texas to her house in California. Now I know that idea is pretty silly, but what isn't silly is the idea that we can control God. And we cannot control the kingdom. Life would be so much easier if we could say enough prayers and jump through enough hoops and, voilá!

I have pretty terrible eyesight. One morning while I was in the Middle East, I pulled off my glasses and they broke in two. The two halves were sitting in my hands. My vision is so bad that I had to get a friend to walk with me a full mile or so to where I could get a bus that would take me to an optometrist; another friend was waiting for me when I got off the bus. Several times people of great faith have prayed for my eyes to be healed, fully believing that God wanted this miracle for me even more than I did. But here I am, still blind as a bat. I know that one day, on this earth, my eyes will be supernaturally healed. But why God hasn't healed them yet, I do not know.

In the kingdom, we are caught up in something that is much greater than we are, something that we cannot control or even fully understand. And we are led by Somebody who is knowable—but not tameable. This Somebody will remain worthy of all of our praises throughout all of eternity. And it is on our praises that His kingdom comes. Genesis 22:14 says, "Abraham called the name of that place The Lord Will Provide, as it is said to this day, 'In the mount of the Lord it will be provided.'" The "mount of the Lord" is Mount Zion. *Zion* means "praise." On the mountain of praises the Lord will provide. I have found that when I need God to supernaturally provide, instead of trying to make myself have enough faith so that heaven will open over me and mountains will move, it's better to turn on some music and praise Him. Life is so much smoother, and my stress level is so much lower, when I don't try to control God or His provision, and instead praise Him for being the Provider, for being good, for being the Lamb who was slain. That praise is actually an expression of faith in His character and ability.

I'm not trying to say that faith can't do incredible things. Without faith it is impossible to please God (see Hebrews 11:6). I'm saying that we cannot control God or His kingdom. "Faith" that tries to believe hard enough in order to manipulate a situation, instead of expressing complete confidence in God, is not faith at all.

It is easier to understand miracles and the realm of the supernatural when we are no longer trying to control the kingdom or fit it into our own way of thinking, but rather accepting it for what it is. I had an extremely painful form of scoliosis for two decades. I played the piano and flute when I was younger, but I had to stop because the pain in my back was so intense. Standing or even sitting for more than an hour or two was a stretch; it didn't take more than fifteen minutes of driving for my back to start hurting. I walked with a limp for several years because the twisting in my spine had actually caused my right leg to become a full inch shorter than my left leg. I even developed TMJ, a painful condition in my jaw that on some days kept me from eating, because my spine was so twisted. Half a dozen pinched nerves at a time was normal for me. When I was eighteen, my doctor told me that I would eventually be in a wheelchair. Considering the constant pain that I was in, I did not doubt it. Physical therapists and chiropractors taught me exercises and strategies for keeping the pain under control, but there is absolutely no cure for scoliosis. The problem does not go away.

When I began to be introduced to the idea of the kingdom of God coming into our own world and setting us free from not only our spiritual infirmities, but also our physical infirmities, I prayed that God would heal my back, and some ministers prayed over it also. I wrestled with God over why I had to live with scoliosis and why He didn't heal me. I asked ministers and close friends, and they didn't have an answer. Then one day I went in for a periodic x-ray and exam. The doctor looked at the images and said, "Wow, that's weird." My spine had straightened, and the nerves and muscles were realigning themselves! God had completely healed my back. I cried the entire way home; then every time I told people what had happened I started crying all over again. Over the next few weeks, as the muscles and nerves in my back realigned themselves, I had less and less pain. I'll never forget the first time I held a baby without any pain. To this day I no longer have pain in my back. The kingdom of God completely overwhelmed the effects of the curse of sin; in this case, it was physical pain and the very real possibility of becoming crippled. That pain is gone. About a month later, I met somebody who also had scoliosis, though not as severe. She asked me to pray for her, and when I did she felt heat in her spine. After that she was completely healed.

But I can't tell you, "Do this and you will be healed." Even great men of faith who have been used to bring healing to countless people cannot tell you the exact formula of how to be healed. But Jesus can. Because it is His kingdom and He is the King. What does He say in the

Lord's prayer? *"Yours* is the kingdom." The kingdom is God's. Jesus is God, not me. And the kingdom is something that He gives to us freely.

It really isn't okay that Satan has authority over the beautiful world that God created. And it certainly isn't okay that he should have any kind of authority over us. The kingdom comes into our lives, stronger and more chaotic than the kingdom of darkness, and reclaims what was lost.

Questions for Discussion/Reflection

1. What are some ways you have seen God's attributes reflected in nature?

2. What does it mean that the kingdom of God is chaotic?

3. What are some ways that the kingdom of God is superior to the kingdom of darkness?

4. The kingdom of God came to earth almost unnoticeably, yet it has been growing uncontrollably for 2,000 years. How have you seen the kingdom in your own life, the lives of those around you, and the world?

5. Have you ever tried to control God? How did that situation turn out?

6. Do you find it scary that we cannot control God or His kingdom? Why or why not?

Chapter 12: Evil for Good

Emily was a single, working mom in her mid-30s. Raising two children alone, while holding a career, was extremely challenging and often very stressful. One particular morning her five-year-old son woke up with a fever. She called her parents and asked if they could watch Ethan for a few hours. She figured that if she got to work on time, at 9:00, she could finish the proposal that was due today and then after lunch be able to finish the day's work at home.

At 8:30 her mom called, saying that she was stuck in traffic and would be a few minutes late. Emily was worried because she would be late to her first meeting. She told her mom that she was going to drive Ethan to the office, so it would be best for her to meet them there, then take Ethan back home. That should give her just enough time to make it to work.

She looked in her rearview mirror at her son, who was curled up against the door and half asleep. "Ethan?" she said, hoping that the stress she was feeling wasn't rubbing off on him. She would hate for him to blame himself for this. "How are you feeling?"

"My tummy has a booboo," he said. A minute later he threw up. Emily pulled over and cleaned him off. She wasn't angry at Ethan for being sick, not by any stretch, but her schedule was very tight. Undoubtedly she would be late.

Just then her phone rang. "Emily, I'm sorry, but I'm still stuck in traffic. It looks like there was a really bad accident at the intersection in front of me. There's emergency workers and everything."

She looked at the clock. It was already 9 o'clock. *Well, I'm already late,* she thought. *I'll just stay at the office later than I planned to try to make up for it.*

Finally, the tower in which she worked came into sight. She glanced at the clock again, hoping that it had moved in reverse. 9:03 a.m. Smoke was rising from the building beside hers. For a moment Emily wondered what was going on, then she screamed as she saw a passenger plane crash into her building.

A few minutes later, when her breathing returned, she looked back at Ethan, who was asleep. "Thank you so much for being sick today," she whispered.

This story about being providentially saved from the September 11th attacks is fictional; I made it up to illustrate the fact that God can take our worst circumstances and use them for our good.

The Story of Joseph

Romans 8:28 says, "And we know that God causes all things to work together for good to those who love God, to those who are called according to His purpose." It does not say that all things are good. Nowhere does the Bible even hint that all things are good. It says that God is working all things together for our good. Joseph's story provides unique insight into finding God in our suffering, and how He ultimately uses our suffering for good. Most children who have been to Sunday school can tell you all about how Joseph's father gave him a coat of many colors. But we like to avoid talking about all of his sufferings and all of the questions about God, evil, and suffering that come with it.

Rachel was Jacob's favorite wife, and her firstborn son, Joseph, was the apple of Jacob's eye. He was the favorite son, and Jacob was not afraid to let everyone else know it. When Joseph was a young man, probably around 17, his father gave him a multi-colored coat as a symbol of his special affection for Joseph. As would be expected, Joseph's eleven brothers were not blind to the favoritism that their father showed him. Being the favorite, and being young, Joseph was a little arrogant. One night he had a dream that his mother, father, and all of his brothers bowed down to him. In youthful cockiness, he told his dream to his family. His brothers did not take it well.

Not long afterward, Jacob sent Joseph to check on his brothers, who were herding sheep in some distant pastures. When they saw him, they plotted to kill him. The oldest of the brothers, Reuben, convinced them not to kill Joseph, but rather throw him in a cistern. Before Reuben could rescue Joseph from the cistern, the others sold him to a group of slave traders. He was taken to Egypt as a slave in the palace of an official named Potiphar.

But God looked with favor on Joseph, and so did Potiphar. He was soon placed in charge of all of the other slaves, until one day, when Potiphar's wife tried to convince Joseph to have sex with her. When Joseph refused and fled, she grabbed his coat and told her husband that Joseph had tried to rape her. Joseph was immediately thrown into prison.

Even in prison, Joseph had favor. When two of Pharoah's men, the cupbearer and the breadmaker, were cast into prison also, Joseph was able to interpret their strange dreams. He correctly interpreted them to mean that in three days the cupbearer would be restored to his position in the palace, but in three days the baker would die. Joseph told the cupbearer to remember him in Pharaoh's palace. He forgot him instead.

Then Pharaoh had a series of strange dreams, and the cupbearer remembered Joseph and his ability to interpret dreams. He told Pharaoh of how Joseph was able to interpret dreams. Joseph was brought from the prison to the palace, and he interpreted Pharaoh's dreams to mean that Egypt would soon experience seven years of plenty, followed by seven years of famine. If you are in doubt as to the severity of a famine and how it can decimate a population, look up pictures of what the recent famine in Somalia has done. That would have been the fate of much of the Middle East, except that Joseph advised Pharoah to put somebody in charge of storing the surplus of grain—that way there would be plenty for the years of famine. The position was given to Joseph.

The famine ravaged the entire Middle East, including Canaan, where Joseph's family was living. Ten of his eleven brothers—all except Benjamin, who was their father's new favorite son—set out for Egypt to buy grain so that they would not starve. When Joseph saw them, he immediately recognized them as his brothers. Believing he was long dead, they did not recognize him. He ordered them to return to their homeland and bring back their youngest brother. They returned with

Benjamin, and Joseph made it appear that young Benjamin had stolen silver from the palace. The brothers were brought before Joseph in the palace, where Joseph revealed himself to them.

At the end of the story, after his trials have finally come to an end and his family had been restored, he said these famous words: "As for you, you meant evil against me, but God meant it for good in order to bring about this present result, to preserve many people alive" (Genesis 50:20).

Where Was God?

A first reading of the story of Joseph can raise more questions than answers about God, evil, and suffering. One that I asked for a long time was: "Who caused Joseph's suffering? Did God cause Joseph to suffer so that eventually he would be able to save the world from famine? Did God *want* him to suffer?" It's easy to see God at the end of the story—when Joseph's suffering is redeemed. But what about while he was in the cistern, while he was a slave, while he was in prison?

God did not cause Joseph's suffering. His father's favoritism and his youthful arrogance combined with his brother's jealousy was a deadly concoction, and one unfortunate event led to another. God was not the author of Joseph's suffering. But because He works all things together for the good of those that love Him, He used Joseph's suffering to help prepare him to save the Middle East and reunite his family. Consider this: it was Joseph and his eleven brothers who were the patriarchs of Israel's twelve tribes. If there was still enmity between them toward the end of their lives, as there was when Joseph was a young man, can you imagine how much the children of Israel would have fought against each other in tribal warfare?

There is no telling how much suffering God spared Joseph. Honestly, it is amazing that he didn't die of some disease or get killed in the prison. When I was in seventh grade, every Wednesday afternoon my friend Ben and I walked the few blocks from our school to our church. There was a busy street that we had to cross. One day right before it was time for us to cross it, I stopped Ben and asked if he wanted to stop at the corner store and get nachos. Just then a car ran through a red light and hit someone who was riding her bike across the street. She was okay, but she broke her arm. If Ben and I wouldn't have paused for a brief moment, it would have been one of us hit by the car, and without a bike to protect us. God spared us from suffering; almost certainly God protected Joseph from murder, disease, a prison insurrection—any number of things.

Could God have rescued Joseph? Yes. Did He? No. You may be struggling with the reality that God very well could have rescued you, or somebody that you love, but for some reason chose not to do so. God had chosen Joseph to save the Middle East from famine, but He could have brought Joseph there some other way. It may not have been necessary for Joseph to suffer all that he did for him to be at Pharoh's palace at the right time for the world to be saved from famine.

Yet I am sure that anybody who has crossed over to the other side of suffering will agree that Joseph's trials helped him develop unshakable confidence in God and the personal character necessary for him to rise to such a high position of power and not seek after personal gain. When we get to heaven, we will know all of the reasons why Joseph suffered so much, and we will have many more answers in regard to our own suffering. We will know exactly what is meant by God using evil for good.

The Early Church

There is one benefit that we have that Joseph did not have, and that is that in the Old Testament the kingdom had not yet come, but now it has. And as I hope you have already begun to see, the kingdom changes everything.

Stoning is truly a horrible death, reserved for those who have brought shame on the community. The person being stoned is not simply knocked unconscious, followed by an easy, painless death. Rather, the entire community, including the person's own family if the crime was shameful enough, gathers in a circle around them and throws stones until the flesh is torn off and there is nothing left but a bloody skeleton. Often the person is not even allowed a proper burial, an additional punishment for bringing shame on the community. Stephen was a follower of Jesus, a citizen of the kingdom, and he was stoned for it. While Stephen was being stoned, he saw heaven open and Jesus standing—not sitting, but standing in honor of him.

Fellow followers of the way wanted to avoid the same fate as Stephen, but as opposition from not only local Jewish factions but also the Roman government grew, it became increasingly difficult. Following Stephen's martyrdom, kingdom citizens spread to the outer reaches and even beyond the borders of the Roman empire, thereby taking the gospel of the kingdom as far as Britain and India. Without Stephen's horrifying death, the gospel may not have spread far beyond the borders of Jerusalem for several years. But because of Stephen's death, the kingdom began to spread through the entire known world. That is why Tertullian, one of the church fathers, said that the blood of the martyrs is the seed of the church.

Paul, who was present at Stephen's stoning and who persecuted the early church, became a follower of the way himself. Because of his faith, he spent years in Roman prisons where he had plenty of time to write letters to churches. Many of his letters became part of the New Testament. On one occasion, a jail warden and his entire family became believers, and on another occasion Paul was brought into Caesar's palace. Of course, he brought the gospel with him. There is no telling how many people became citizens of the kingdom, largely as a result of Paul's sufferings. Or rather, because, like Joseph, he decided to follow God in the midst of his suffering.

The kingdom is God's answer to evil and suffering. As you saw in this chapter, the kingdom brings good out of our suffering. In the next few chapters, you will see how the kingdom ultimately provides a way out of suffering.

Questions for Discussion/Reflection

1. Have you ever been in a situation like Emily's, when something bad happened but it spared you from a much greater evil?

2. Have bad things in your life made you doubt that God works all things together for your good? What insight can you draw from Joseph's story to help ease your doubts?

3. In the midst of unspeakable circumstances, God looked with favor on Joseph. How has God looked with favor on you?

4. What does it mean that God uses evil for good?

5. Joseph didn't have the kingdom, but we do. How does this change things for us?

6. What does it mean that the kingdom is God's answer to evil and suffering?

Chapter 13: Evil and the Glory of God

In the last chapter, some interesting questions were raised about God's role in Joseph's suffering. Does God cause suffering? Does God want us to suffer? The answers to these questions are extremely important, because they really determine whether or not we can trust Him. Spoiler: We *can* trust Him.

I am not equipped to fully answer all of the questions associated with evil, suffering, and the goodness of God. Probably a lot more questions have been raised than answered. But throughout this book, especially in the previous chapter and this one, I hope to give you the tools to begin answering these questions in a way that is biblically solid and meaningful to you on a personal level.

Is Evil Necessary?

Here's a tricky question that could be easily glossed over. But it's one that I have asked many times, and many others ask it as well. Why? Because we want the answer. And we know that the answer will tell us a lot about the character and nature of God, as well as the world that we live in.

In asking if evil is necessary, we need to qualify this by asking— *necessary for what?* For man to have free will? Adam and Eve had free will before they ate from the forbidden tree. For us to appreciate God? Small children who are still oblivious to evil are able to show deep appreciation for the goodness and love that their parents show them. But at the same time, there is definitely a deeper appreciation for God after walking through suffering.

So the question remains—is evil necessary for God to be glorified? I majored in theology at a conservative Southern Baptist college, and

I have friends who majored in theology at similar colleges, and every one of us agree that if we were taking a test and didn't know the answer, we could say, "For the glory of God," and automatically get it correct. Did Jesus have the ability to sin, or did He just never sin? Write a long paragraph about the glory of God through the life of Jesus. Why is the gospel of John so different from the Synoptic Gospels? Because the glory of God is seen in diversity. If you are currently studying theology or planning to in the near future, this is an easy way to an A+. It's almost like a theological cop-out. Unless you take a closer look at what the glory of God really is.

A Closer Look at the Glory of God

The most visible example of the manifest glory of God is found in the Old Testament, when the presence of God came to rest over the mercy seat of the ark of the covenant in the Old Testament. The ark of the covenant was an elegant box made of acacia wood and overlaid with gold. Inside, it contained the stone tablets with the Ten Commandments, Aaron's staff that budded, and a jar of manna. Each of these things served as a reminder of God's presence among the Israelites during their flight from Egypt and their wandering in the desert. On the lid of the ark were two cherubim who faced each other and whose wings touched each other. There, between the cherubim, the glory of God came to rest—His visible, manifest presence among the people.

The ark of the covenant was actually an altar, and an altar is first and foremost a place of sacrifice. Located in the Holy of Holies, the inner sanctum of the temple, it was on the ark of the covenant that once a year the High Priest would make an animal sacrifice, as prescribed by the Law, for the sins of the people. This sacrifice would cover the sins of the people for the year. For this reason, the lid to the ark was known as the atonement cover or the mercy seat. It was here, on this place of sacrifice and reconciliation, that the glory of God came to dwell.

There I will meet with you; and from above the mercy seat, from between the two cherubim which are upon the ark of the testimony [covenant], I will speak to you about all that I will give you in commandment for the sons of Israel (Exodus 25:22).

Now when Moses went into the tent of meeting to speak with Him, he heard the voice speaking to him from above the mercy seat that was on the ark of the testimony [covenant], from between the two cherubim, so He spoke to him (Numbers 7:89).

These verses make it clear that the purpose of the presence over the ark of the covenant, the manifest glory of God, was that God could meet with man. So when we talk about the glory of God, we are essentially talking about His meeting with us!

Hundreds of years later, after splitting into the two kingdoms of Israel and Judah, the Israelites were carried into exile by the Assyrians for their idolatry and rebellion. Not long afterward, the kingdom of Judah was given over to the Babylonians and the Jews went into exile. It was in Babylon that Ezekiel was called to be a prophet to the exiles. In Ezekiel 10, the prophet recounts what had to be the worst day of his life. In a vision, he saw the presence of God over the ark of the covenant leave.

After seventy years of captivity in Babylon, the Jews were allowed to return to their homeland, which was now in complete disrepair. When Cyrus allowed them to return, they set to rebuilding the temple. But the ark of the covenant was no longer in their possession. It is believed that it was either carried off into Babylon or hidden. To this day, nobody knows where the ark of the covenant is.

The Jews had suffered immensely while in captivity, and they were determined to not let it happen again. They were not going to reject the law of God again. So the people took the Mosaic law and added law upon law to it. It was as if in adding extra laws they were building a fence around the law, ensuring that it would not be broken. The problem was that the ark of the covenant was no longer there. The sacred altar of sacrifice and reconciliation, which housed the glory of God, was gone. So they did what so many of us are guilty of doing—they traded the glory of God for legalism. They carried on like this for the next 400 years. There are no biblical writings to cover this 400-year period between Malachi and Matthew. Theologians refer to it as the 400 years of silence, because during this time the people did not hear the voice of

God. The presence had left. Not until Jesus, who was the image of the invisible God, came to earth was God's voice heard again. The night before His crucifixion, Jesus said:

> "The hour has come for the Son of Man to be glorified. Truly, truly, I say to you, unless a grain of wheat falls into the earth and dies, it remains alone; but if it dies, it bears much fruit. He who loves his life loses it, and he who hates his life in this world will keep it to life eternal. If anyone serves Me, he must follow Me; and where I am, there My servant will be also; if anyone serves Me, the Father will honor him. Now My soul has become troubled; and what shall I say, 'Father, save Me from this hour'? But for this purpose I came to this hour. Father, glorify Your name." Then a voice came out of heaven: "I have both glorified it, and will glorify it again" (John 12:23-28).

Through Jesus' death, God would be glorified because He would once again be meeting with man, but through a new covenant that is far superior to the old one. A massive curtain, sixty feet high and four inches thick, guarded the entrance into the Holy of Holies and symbolized the separation between man and God. When Jesus breathed His last breath, the curtain was torn. The separation between man and God was gone, and man could once again meet with God. Now with our hearts as an altar, His presence comes into our lives and His glory is revealed through us.

Do you remember the promise found in Eve's name, which means, "the mother of all living"? Through Jesus' death, man could meet with God and therefore be made fully alive. And as Irenaeus said, the glory of God is man fully alive. Jesus suffered the greatest evil for our greatest good. The curse on Satan, given in Genesis 3, was completed when Jesus took his authority from him. The kingdom of God came to earth, and as it began to permanently change people's hearts and lives, the kingdom of darkness began to lose dominion.

Is evil necessary for God to be glorified? God was perfectly complete in all of His glory before creating the world, but He chose to set His image—you and me—on the earth to become the vessels of His glory. God was glorified through His perfect communion with Adam and Eve before they ate the forbidden fruit. But they ate the forbidden fruit. Evil became a part of everyone's life. And through the most evil act in all of history, God's glory is revealed to its fullest.

John Piper said, "Sin killed itself when it killed Jesus."[10] The crucifixion of Jesus was the most evil act in all of history. It was the sum of every evil act ever committed. And on the cross, evil committed suicide.

Personally, I don't believe that evil is necessary. But it is what we have in this post-Genesis 3, pre-Revelation 20 world. And the God who was able to take the evil that was done to His Son and make something beautiful out of it—the same God who saved the Middle East from famine because Joseph's sufferings had led him to the right place at just the right time—can reveal Himself in your most tragic circumstances. Just watch and see.

Questions for Discussion/Reflection

1. Oftentimes in the midst of suffering, we use platitudes such as, "Perhaps it's best this way." How do these platitudes make you feel?

2. On a personal level, what does it mean that the "glory of God is man fully alive"?

3. What are some ways that God was glorified through Jesus' death?

4. Do you feel that evil is necessary for God to be glorified? Why or why not?

---

10. John Piper, "How Did God Make Evil Commit Suicide At the Cross?" Desiring God, December 1, 2008, http://www.desiringgod.org/resource-library/ask-pastor-john/how-did-god-make-evil-commit-suicide-at-the-cross.

Chapter 14: Redemption

Most of us can probably say that when we are suffering, we want God to rescue us. We want Him to supernaturally cause our suffering to end. And a lot of times, He does. There are plenty of reports, even today, of supernatural miracles that leave doctors dumbfounded, and stories so full of coincidences that they have to come straight from heaven.

But sometimes, He doesn't rescue us. A great example of this is found in the story of Lazarus. Mary and Martha sent a messenger to Jesus to tell Him that their brother, whom Jesus loved, was sick. Jesus responded to this by *waiting*. Instead of hurrying to Lazarus's bedside to miraculously cure his sickness, He waited in Jerusalem for two days before setting out for the village of Bethany. By the time He left, Lazarus had already died.

Mary and Martha both gave the heartbroken response, "If only You had been here, my brother would not have died" (see John 11:21,32). But in the midst of their tragedy, they began to see the love that Jesus had for Lazarus. He began to cry. The Jews standing nearby said, "See how much He loved him!" If we ask God to open our eyes while we are in pain, we will find that Jesus is right there with us and we will see with even more fullness and clarity how much He loves us.

Mary and Martha knew that Jesus had the power to cure sickness, but they didn't realize that He had the power to raise the dead. They got a miracle—one much bigger than the one they had hoped for. Mary and Martha saw their brother come back to life. In this, they saw an even greater manifestation of the person of Jesus of Nazareth, and the glory of God was more fully revealed than it would have been if Jesus had simply healed their brother's sickness.

Many of us are looking to God for a rescue, but what He has to offer is much greater. He is offering a redemption. He wants to show us more of who He is and more of how precious we are to Him. God's unchanging character is one of redemption.

Jesus could have healed Lazarus's illness and prevented him from dying, and they would have seen the power and glory of God manifested through Him. But because He waited and performed an even greater miracle, many people put their faith in Him.

Finding Our Value

Redemption means that something finds its value. For example, if I have a ten-dollar bill, it is worth nothing on its own. It is only a glorified piece of paper, specially designed to go through the washing machine and come out unscathed (ask me how I know this). I can't eat it (ask me how I know this too). I can't drink it. It cannot meet any of my basic needs. But a ten-dollar bill finds its value when I go to the grocery store and use it to buy food.

What God is offering us is a relationship with Him in which we find what we are truly worth. When the car that I drove in college finally broke down, I thought that the man at the junkyard should give me $2,000 for it. That's what I thought it was worth. I got $500. What was the car really worth? Even though I thought it was worth $2,000, it was only worth $500. Something's worth is always determined by what a person is willing to pay for it.

Do you remember Rachel's story from the first chapter? She looks exactly like her father. For some people, it is a treasure to look like their parents. But as a young adult, she looked in the mirror and only saw a prisoner's defiled daughter. Despite all her theological knowledge, she truly believed that she was worthless. But her worth is not defined by a child rapist or her father's criminal behavior. Her worth is determined by what Jesus was willing to pay for her.

Jacob's first wife, Leah, lived in the shadow of her younger sister, Rachel. Rachel was beautiful in form and lovely, but Leah was unpleasant to look at. When Jacob came to work for her father, Laban, he vowed seven years of work for Rachel's hand in marriage. But Laban knew that nobody would want to marry Leah, so he tricked Jacob into marrying her instead. How do you think that make Leah feel? "You're too ugly for anybody to want to marry you, but I think that I can trick your cousin into marrying you so that I can get you off my hands."

To add insult to injury, he acted as if Rachel was his wife. "So Jacob went in to Rachel also, and indeed he loved Rachel more than Leah, and he served with Laban for another seven years" (Genesis 29:30). All in all, Jacob worked fourteen years for Rachel, while Leah was cast aside by both her father and her husband.

Leah looked to her father to find her value, and she found nothing. Then she looked to her husband for her value and found nothing yet again. So she did what any other woman in her situation would do. She started having as many children as she possibly could.

Now the Lord saw that Leah was unloved, and He opened her womb, but Rachel was barren. Leah conceived and bore a son and named him Reuben, for she said, "Because the Lord has seen my affliction; surely now my husband will love me." Then she conceived again and bore a son and said, "Because the Lord has heard that I am unloved, He has therefore given me this son also." So she named him Simeon. She conceived again and bore a son and said, "Now this time my husband will become attached to me, because I have borne him three sons." Therefore he was named Levi (Genesis 29:31-34).

In a sense, Leah was now looking for her value from her children. She wanted her children to prove to her husband, and to herself, that she was valuable. And again, she found nothing. Yet she soon realized where her value comes from. "And she conceived again and bore a son and said, 'This time I will praise the Lord.' Therefore she named him Judah. Then she stopped bearing" (Genesis 29:35).

The name *Judah* actually means "praise," and it was from the relationship with God that she found and from the overflow of her praise that she found her worth. And her worth was immense. It was through Judah that the Messiah came. Did you catch that? Leah, unlovely and unloved Leah, not Rachel, was the forerunner of the Messiah.

Leah wanted to be rescued, but what God had to offer her was much greater. Sometimes He withholds rescue to bring about redemption. Redemption is about God bringing about a greater miracle so that in the process He is revealed to more people.

Restoring That Which Was Lost

Naomi left the land of Bethlehem with her husband and two sons because there was a famine in the land and they were in danger of starvation. They went across the Jordan River, which helped mark the boundary of Israel, to the land of Moab, where her sons married Moabite women. Upon the death of her husband and sons, and hearing that there was now bread in Bethlehem, Naomi and her daughter-in-law Ruth set out for Israel. But Naomi was a different person than when she left. The women of Bethlehem said, "Could this be Naomi?" Naomi's name meant "lovely." But her response was that her name was no longer Naomi; her name was Mara because her life has become bitter. Undoubtedly she had waited for God to rescue her. He had not. He had something much bigger and better in mind.

Naomi still had Ruth, and she loved Ruth like a daughter. Ruth and Naomi worked in the fields so they were able to eat and survive. But Naomi wanted more for Ruth than survival. She wanted Ruth to remarry and become prosperous. Following Naomi's advice, Ruth was able to marry Boaz, the owner of the field in which they worked. Boaz was also her kinsman-redeemer, which means that he was a male relative with the right and responsibility to assist a relative in need. They had a son, Obed, and Naomi helped raise him. In fact, it was said of Naomi that she was given another son! Her joy was restored.

But the story does not end there. Obed was the father of Jesse, the father of David, who became the greatest king of Israel. It was prophesied that David would never fail to have a king sit on his throne, and that prophecy was fulfilled when Jesus, the Messiah, was born from the line of David. Jesus is our Kinsman-Redeemer, because, being found in the likeness of man and therefore in a sense a blood relation to us, He was given the privilege and responsibility of assisting us in our need. He did this by paying the price of sin through His death on the cross; marrying the widow of God's judgment, the church; executing vengeance on the Devil; and bringing us back to perfect communion with God. Not only was Naomi's life restored, but in guiding Ruth and helping to raise Obed, she played an important role in the restoration of all humanity.

In the book of Joel, God makes an incredible promise: "Then I will make up to you for the years that the swarming locust has eaten" (Joel 2:25).

A Double Portion

Let's take a look at what a double portion means. In ancient Middle Eastern culture, and to an extent in modern Middle Eastern culture, when a father died he left all of his property to his sons in equal shares. However, the oldest son received two of those shares. This was not because of favoritism; it was because of the responsibility that fell to the eldest son. As the new man of the house, it was now his job to care for his mother and any children who had not yet grown up. He also had to carry on the family trade. These responsibilities required extra resources, which is why the oldest son was given the most. Likewise, when God blesses us, there is a degree of responsibility attached to that blessing. If it is a financial blessing, we should give at least a tenth of it to kingdom work. If it is the blessing of marriage, children, etc., we should also use that blessing to bless others.

But there is more to God's blessing than simply receiving an extra share to carry out our kingdom responsibilities. Look at what happened to Job at the end of his unspeakable sufferings. After Job prayed for his friends, the Lord made him prosperous again and gave him twice as much as he had before. The Lord blessed the latter part of Job's life more than the first (see Job 42:10,12). Before losing everything, Job was one of the wealthiest men of his day. *And God gave him twice as much as he had before.* Not because God was somehow apologizing for how much Job had suffered, or even because He had a job for Job to do, but simply because of His love and faithfulness.

It is common, especially among men, to derive a great degree of their identity from wealth and the status that it brings. There is no reason to believe that Job was different, or didn't at least struggle under that temptation. But I am sure that at the end of his suffering, Job's perspective toward his own wealth had changed. He no longer considered it as something that was rightfully his, but as a gift from God. Before his suffering, when somebody commented on his wealth, he may have felt a bit of pride and wanted to show them the extent of his vast riches. But afterward, when his wealth was even greater, if somebody commented on it, I imagine he may have simply smiled and acknowledged that it was not really his, but God's. And it is much better for it to be in God's hands instead of his.

So how much did Job gain? I said in the prologue of this book that in the beginning, God was proving Job to Satan, but in the end we find that all along God was proving Himself to Job. Apart from becoming immeasurably wealthy, Job gained sight of God (see Job 42:5). And that alone was enough.

The Pearl of Great Price

Most of you probably know how pearls are formed. When a piece of sand gets caught in an oyster, it irritates the oyster so much that it secretes a substance to coat the sand. Eventually it turns into a pearl. Pearls are very unique among jewels in that they are the only jewel that comes from a wound. That is perhaps the most perfect example of how a rescue is denied, but something greater is brought about. In the Bible, there are several references to pearls. In Matthew 13:45-46, Jesus tells a parable of a merchant seeking fine pearls. When he finds one, he sells everything he owns to buy it. Revelation 21:21 says that the twelve gates of heaven are each made of a single pearl.

Finding God in the midst of suffering is like finding a treasure of unspeakable value. When His love comes and fills the emptiness created by divorce or abortion or any number of things, He is taking that wound and creating a jewel.

The gates of heaven are made of a single pearl. That pearl is Jesus. It is because of His wounds and the beauty that flows from them that we have gained entrance into the kingdom of God. And when we hand Him our wounds, even though it may be the most costly offering we ever give Him, He fills them with His love and turns them into pearls. We hand Him our wounds, and in return He gives us pearls.

My grandmother is a classic Southern belle from Mississippi. When I was in college, she told me that every woman needs a pearl necklace in order to really feel like a lady. And I believe that in this fallen and broken world, rather than having a perfect life free from suffering, what we all need is a few pearls to show the world the beauty of our King.

> Therefore we do not lose heart, but though our outer man is decaying, yet our inner man is being renewed day by day. For momentary, light affliction is producing for us an eternal weight of glory far beyond all comparison, while we look not at the things which are seen, but at the things which are not seen; for the things which are seen are temporal, but the things which are not seen are eternal (2 Corinthians 4:16-18).

The renewal that Paul is talking about in this verse is the renewal of our hearts that happens when we trade in ashes and receive beauty, when we give Him a wound and He gives us a pearl.

All of these stories that I have used—Leah, Naomi, and Job—are from the Old Testament. Because Jesus had not come yet; neither had the kingdom. They did not get to experience what you and I get to experience. Leah and Naomi were privileged to be in the lineage of Jesus, but we get to actually know Jesus. All of the Old Testament believers will get to see Jesus in heaven, but we get to see Him on earth. And we have the privilege of becoming like Him, not only in His death, but also in His resurrection. We are privileged to live with the curse of sin over our lives broken. Because of Jesus and the kingdom that He brought with Him, we can have a great deal more than the greatest of the Old Testament believers.

Where Redemption Begins

It is easy to fall into the trap of seeking after all the blessings of God, such as a double portion for our suffering and redemption of all we have lost, instead of seeking first His kingdom. But may we never forget that the real blessing is found in seeking not His hand, but His face. "The whole work of God in redemption is to undo the tragic effects of [the Fall], and to bring us back again into right and eternal relationship with Himself. This requires that our sins be disposed of satisfactorily, that a full reconciliation be effected, and the way opened for us to return again into conscious communion with God and to live again in the Presence, as before [the Fall]."[11] Living in the manifest presence of God is where redemption begins; otherwise we become like the man who gains the world yet forfeits his own soul.

Questions for Discussion/Reflection

1. In what ways can you personally relate to the story of Lazarus?

2. Name a time when you felt like Leah. What are you really worth? How do you know that?

3. When have you seen God make a pearl?

4. What is something in your own life that you are waiting for God to restore?

---

11. A.W. Tozer and Samuel Marinus Zwemer, *The Pursuit of God* (Harrisburg, PA: Christian Publications, 1948), 33. Public Domain.

5. Have you ever seen God give somebody a double portion? Why do you think He did it? All things considered, how much did that person gain?

6. In what ways are you seeking the blessings of God rather than seeking His face? In what ways are you seeking His face over His blessings?

Chapter 15: The Grander Design

Have you ever heard the expression, "He missed the forest for the trees"? This means that somebody got so caught up in the details that they missed the big picture. If you have ever gone for a walk through a forest, you probably think of it as a jumbled mess of strewn tree leaves, roots, trees, and small plants. But the branching of every tree, the veins on every leaf, even the skin of snakes and frogs and other animals exhibit complex fractal patterns. If you were in a helicopter and caught a bird's eye view of that same forest that from the ground looks like complete disorder, you would see something entirely different. You wouldn't see a random conglomeration or straight lines and rows of trees. You would see something far more beautiful and complex.

While we typically think of chaos as a lack of order, chaos is actually an order that is far greater than we are able to recognize or even imagine. In the end, when the grander scheme begins to be unravelled, we see how God really was working everything together for our good and how He does make everything beautiful in its own time. It is like watching from the other side while an artist creates a tapestry. All that is seen from the other side of the weaving is the knots from tying the string. But when the material is turned over, the picture is revealed, and it is overwhelmingly beautiful. Desmond Tutu, the South African archbishop who fought against apartheid, said, "Out of the cacophony of random suffering and chaos that can mark human life, the life artist sees or creates a symphony of meaning and order."

Putting the Pieces Together

Have you ever felt that your life is like a jigsaw puzzle and there are far too many disparate pieces to even think about where they should go? The chaos of life can make it hard to imagine that any of the pieces should fit together at all.

Think of a jigsaw puzzle you get from the store. When you open it and empty all of the 500 or 1,500 or 2,000 pieces on the table, the task ahead of you seems large indeed. All the pieces need to be turned over so that the picture is showing; the border pieces need to be separated from the inner pieces; the four corners need to be found—all before you even begin to put the pieces together. Sometimes putting all of the pieces together can take weeks or even months. But the final picture is always more stunning than the picture on the box.

We are not supposed to put the broken pieces of our lives together. It's pretty much impossible when there's 2,000 pieces of yourself lying around, and you don't even have the box with the picture on it to know what the finished product is supposed to look like. But God does. And He can take all of the broken pieces and fit them together perfectly. When He is done, the puzzle that was your life is now a crucial piece of an even larger puzzle.

Doomsday Eschatology

How many books and movies can you think of about the end times? For the past few decades Christians as a culture have been obsessed with the idea that the country's failing morality and the church's defensive position are signs that the end is near. I was actually taught that the formation of global bodies such as the United Nations, which has done incredible good for the world's poorest people, and the fact that we are given social security numbers at birth are signs that the end is near. As a child, I knew a couple who constantly said, "The rapture is going to happen before such and such...." The rapture will happen before their then 5-year-old grandson learned how to drive...the rapture will happen before I graduate college, so on and so forth. All of their predictions were false. But because of their obsession with the end times, I was filled with such an impending sense of doom that I refused to think about anything beyond high school. We know that the end is near and Jesus could come back any day because of how terrible the world has become. Doom and gloom surely must surround the second coming of Jesus. Right? Wrong.

It is true that the chaotic rule of sin has wreaked havoc on this world and caused an untold amount of devastation. But the Bible says in Isaiah 9:7 that the increase of the rule of the kingdom of Jesus Christ will have no end. In other words, His kingdom is going to keep growing and growing and it is not going to slow down. And the kingdom of darkness has to submit to the kingdom of God! The kingdom of God has been and always will be far superior. How can we be worried about the Antichrist when we have the Christ?

Things may seem as if they are going from bad to worse in America with the economy, national politics, education, housing, global warming, etc. But what about all of the things that are improving? Only a century ago food could not be stored in refrigerators or freezers. Scientific achievements have virtually eradicated diseases such as polio and measles. People from the early 1900s who had polio or the Spanish flu would probably look at us with our national struggle over poor food choices and the ensuing diseases, like type two diabetes, and shake their heads, saying, "*That* is your health crisis?" Tell someone who experienced the Great Depression and World War II that the world is worse off now. And while it may seem that in America the church is on the defensive, in places such as Africa, the Middle East, and the Far East people are entering the kingdom in droves. The reign of Jesus is continually expanding, exactly as was prophesied.

No More Curse

Remember that in the middle of the garden of Eden there were two trees? There wasn't only the forbidden Tree of the Knowledge of Good and Evil. There was also the Tree of Life. After Adam and Eve were cast out of the garden, an angel with a flaming sword was placed at the entrance. The angel was not there to prevent anyone else from eating the fruit of the Tree of the Knowledge of Good and Evil. Genesis 3:24 says, "So He drove the man out; and at the east of the garden of Eden He stationed the cherubim and the flaming sword which turned every direction to guard the way to the *tree of life*." The angel was there to keep humankind from eating from the Tree of Life. Why? Because sin had already descended on God's perfect world; in God's mercy, He refused to let us live forever in a world overrun with disease, death, poverty, and every other evil that you see on the evening news.

Do you remember how it was God who gave the curse in Genesis 3, and that it was actually an act of mercy to help us recognize our need for Him? A day is coming when the curse will be completely gone. "And He will wipe away every tear from their eyes; and there will no longer be any death; there will no longer be any mourning, or crying, or pain; the first things have passed away" (Revelation 21:4). At this time, the curse of sin is entirely erased. Pain, sorrow, and death are all listed in the curse in Genesis 3. In heaven, they will all be eradicated.

Nikki was the young woman, mentioned in the first chapter, who lived at one of the Roloff homes and was told that God would kill her brothers to make her repent. For many years, Revelation 21:4 was her favorite verse. After the Roloff homes were closed down and she was sent to another foster home, she met several other foster children who also claimed this verse as their favorite. These children had already suffered unspeakably in their short lives, and many of them cried themselves to sleep every night. But this verse gave them hope that one day their suffering really would end. But there is much more than suffering finally coming to an end.

And He who sits on the throne said, "Behold, I am making all things new." And He said, "Write, for these words are faithful and true" (Revelation 21:5).

Then he showed me a river of the water of life, clear as crystal, coming from the throne of God and of the Lamb, in the middle of its street. On either side of the river was the tree of life, bearing twelve kinds of fruit, yielding its fruit every month; and the leaves of the tree were for the healing of the nations. There will no longer be any curse; and the throne of God and of the Lamb will be in it, and His bond-servants will serve Him (Revelation 22:1-3).

The Tree of Life is back. God loves us too much to let us live forever in this fallen, sinful world, but He wants us to live forever with Him in heaven.

Questions for Discussion/Reflection

1. What does it mean that chaos is an order grander than we are able to recognize?

2. In talking about jigsaw puzzles, this chapter says that our lives are a piece of an even larger puzzle. What do you think that larger puzzle is?

3. What does the Bible say about the end times? How does that measure against what you know about God's character?

4. One day the curse will be completely eradicated. How does this affect your perception of God, evil, suffering, and your own life?

Part 4: Our Response to Evil and Suffering

Chapter 16: Partnering With God

In the 1800s and early 1900s, the Western world experienced a movement called the Social Gospel. The backbone of the Social Gospel movement was putting into practice Matthew 6:10: "Your kingdom come. Your will be done, on earth as it is in heaven." Proponents of the Social Gospel were reformers who sought to bring an end to social evils such as extreme poverty, child labor, and inadequate schools. Settlement homes, such as Hull House in Chicago, provided housing and social services to the extremely poor. Pastors began churches in places like Hell's Kitchen in New York City. Some Social Gospelers were active on the Underground Railroad and in helping former slaves have a chance at a better life.

Many middle- and upper-class Christians denounced the Social Gospel, claiming that focusing on social aid was a distraction to preaching the Word of God. But in the ministry of Jesus, the good news always came hand in hand with meeting a person's expressed need. In fact, the gospel is about meeting our deepest need. An orphan's deepest need is to know that he or she is loved. What does the gospel say about that? A lot! In John 14:18 Jesus says, "I will not leave you as orphans." James 1:27 says, "Pure and undefiled religion in the sight of our God and Father is this: to visit orphans and widows in their distress, and to keep oneself unstained by the world." The need of the sick is healing. Jesus performed numerous healings to demonstrate His ability to meet the needs of the sick, both physically and spiritually. In fact, when John the Baptist sent his disciples to ask Jesus if He really was the Messiah, Jesus' response was, "The blind receive sight and the lame walk, the lepers are cleansed and the deaf hear, the dead are raised up, and the poor have the gospel preached to them" (Matthew 11:5). The proof that

Jesus was the Messiah was the miracles that were happening; people's deepest needs were being met.

Preaching the gospel while offering no help to the injustices and sufferings that a person is facing truncates the true message of Jesus. A sick person being healed or an orphan being loved is not the equivalent of salvation. But it opens their eyes to the true character of a God who loves them.

Passivity

Passivity refers to inactivity, usually waiting for another person to step up to the plate. A passive person is lacking energy or will.

William Carey is considered the father of modern missions. During his early years, before heading off to India, he faced much discouragement and pessimism from those around him. At one point a church minister said to him, "Young man, when God desires to convert the heathen, He will do it without your help or mine." This man not only lacked concern for unreached peoples, he also did not understand that God desires to use us to fulfill the Great Commission.

After performing the greatest act in the history of the universe, Jesus left everything to His eleven remaining disciples. What if they failed? He had no plan B. Of course, He could have carried out the task of bringing the gospel to every nation by Himself. But it was God's plan, which we know by faith is perfect, that we partner with Him to bring the world to redemption.

This doesn't mean that God is sitting on His hands waiting for us to become bold enough to begin evangelizing. Most people today who are entering the kingdom of God are from a Muslim background. They are having dreams about Jesus. I have spent a lot of time with Muslims who are having dreams about Jesus. It really is amazing. God could do this all by Himself. But He chooses to do it with us.

From Preschoolers to Partners

When we first enter the kingdom of God, we are like young children who need to be constantly nurtured and taught basic things such as obedience and the holiness of God. We're like preschoolers who need to learn that hitting and biting are not acceptable forms of communication. (How many of us still hit and bite within the church?) We must learn to respect those in authority over us. Think of when extended family comes together to enjoy the holidays; at mealtimes there may be two separate tables—one for the kids and one for the adults. It's not at all a bad thing. Some of my best childhood memories come from sitting at the kids' table. Our plates were prepared for us and the food was usually cut into small pieces, because we were not capable of passing hot dishes around the table or using a knife without an emergency room visit. Usually the kids' table was outside, so we could talk as loud as we wanted. My cousins and I would tell knock-knock jokes and funny stories about our pets and how to make good prank phone calls. The maturity and the level of thinking we had as five-year-olds were not anywhere near a level in which we would have enjoyed sitting at the table with aunts, uncles, and grandparents discussing world events.

But we don't have to remain as young children. As children grow up, they move from a relationship in which their parents and caregivers are constantly meeting their needs and making decisions for them to a more mature one in which they enjoy the company of their superiors. They are able to help make important decisions, and while their level of thinking is not on the same level as that of an adult, their input is appreciated. The child gets to move from the kids' table to the adults' table and can partake in, and contribute to, adult conversation. They don't need their parents any less; they still need nurturing and affirmation. Those needs will never go away, even in adulthood. But instead of having their plates prepared and their food cut for them before they are sent outside, they are now becoming a part of the adult world. Not all children have the privilege of having parents who want to enjoy their company as young adults. If you are having a hard time with this image, think of a special relative or an adult in your life who has been very important. How has your relationship with this person changed since you were young?

A Theology of Chaos

There are several people in the Bible who reached this level of maturity with God, in which they were able to contribute to His decisions. Instead of simply doing what they were told to do, they used their own personalities and gifts to partner with God. Abraham was one of them. The first thing we are told about Abraham is that he was incredibly obedient. When God told him to leave his homeland and go to the land that He would show him, Abraham got up and left. This obedience laid the foundation for a partnership with God. When God was preparing to destroy Sodom and Gomorrah, He said, "Shall I hide from Abraham what I am about to do?" (Genesis 18:17). He told Abraham and allowed him to be a part of the decision. Abraham convinced God that if there were enough righteous people living in Sodom and Gomorrah, He should not destroy it!

Another such person was Moses. When the Israelites worshiped the golden calf, God said that He would destroy them and make Moses into a mighty nation instead of them. Moses spoke with God and reminded Him of His promise to Abraham, Isaac, and Jacob; then God relented from destroying the Israelites. Some translations even say that God changed His mind. Does this mean that God is uncertain or that He does not do what He has set out to do? Absolutely not! It means that Moses had so much favor with God that He was given a "spiritual promotion." Instead of sitting at the kids' table, he was allowed to sit at the adults' table and contribute to God's plan for the nation. This isn't favoritism. It's maturity.

If we find ourselves in a place where we are asking God to fix a problem, He might respond, "You fix it." It's not because He doesn't want to fix the problem. It's because He wants to fix it with you.

When disasters such as tsunamis and earthquakes strike and whole nations find themselves in a state of chaos, it is not necessarily the job of the government to come to the rescue. It is first and foremost the responsibility of God's people. We have the privilege and responsibility of showing the rest of the world what hope looks like. We get to be the hands and feet of Jesus. He equips us and empowers us to carry His Name into inner city neighborhoods filled with the chaos of gang violence, drug abuse, and unemployment, and into disaster areas full of their own chaos, hundreds or even thousands of miles away.

The Offering of Everything

Now one of the Pharisees was requesting Him to dine with him, and He entered the Pharisee's house and reclined at the table. And there was a woman in the city who was a sinner; and when she learned that He was reclining at the table in the Pharisee's house, she brought an alabaster vial of perfume, and standing behind Him at His feet, weeping, she began to wet His feet with her tears, and kept wiping them with the hair of her head, and kissing His feet and anointing them with the perfume (Luke 7:36-38).

The Pharisee who had invited Jesus to dinner said that if Jesus was a prophet, surely He would know that the woman who was touching Him was sinful. In John's account of this story, those around thought that what she did was a huge waste.

What I find so beautiful about this story is that this woman counted the cost, and she found that Jesus was worth everything. She did not hesitate to give Him everything in one loving act. If we are holding anything back, it is because we have not begun to see His worth.

This kind of love for Jesus overflows as a deep and genuine love for the people created in His image and a strong desire to stand for and defend the decrees of the King. True love for Jesus causes us to be unable to tolerate injustice. We partner with the King of Kings to extend His rule of peace and justice and help end suffering.

Larry and Jean Elliot, Karen Watson, and David and Carrie McDonnall were working on a water purification project in Mosul, Iraq in March of 2003. They knew what they were getting into when they packed their bags and headed to a nation devastated by Saddam Hussein's regime and the war that followed September 11, 2001. And Jesus was worth it. His image on the faces of Iraqis made it worth leaving everything, knowing that they may not come back. Then one day the barrel of a machine gun poked through the window of their car. All except for Carrie were killed. "Why do some people who 'have it made' mess up their comfort zone to stand up for some poor soul who is being abused? Most people know the difference between right and wrong. But royal people [sons and daughters of King Jesus] have a powerful sense of justice in the depths of their souls that drives them to act when they see something wrong."[12]

Nate Saint, Ed McCully, Peter Leming, and Jim Elliott were in Ecuador with their wives and children. Their goal was to bring the gospel to the Huaorani, one of the most violent tribes in South America. The Huaorani were so isolated that they had virtually no chance to hear the gospel. When the men finally approached them, they were speared to death. Before heading to South America, Jim Elliot showed much promise as a Bible teacher, and he was urged to stay in the United States. Instead he went to a completely unreached people. And he was killed for it.

Many people have died in the pursuit of expanding the King's rule. Many others, such as Amy Carmichael and Mother Teresa, did not die as martyrs, but still gave their lives to serving the poor. Some would look at their lives, and their deaths, and say that it was all a waste. But Jesus receives the offerings of their lives as the alabaster jar of perfume that was broken over His feet. And if you read about the lives of missionaries, what you find over and over and over again is that their love for Jesus turned into an irresistible love for people.

Questions for Discussion/Reflection

1. Why is it important that we preach the gospel while meeting people's needs?

2. What is passivity? Why is it wrong for kingdom citizens to be passive?

12. Kris Vallotton and Bill Johnson, *The Supernatural Ways of Royalty* (Shippensburg, PA: Destiny Image, 2006), 139-140.

3. In what ways are you still a preschooler in God's family? In what ways are you maturing? What would it look like for you to reach the level of maturity with God that Abraham and Moses reached?

4. Name some people who offered everything to Jesus.

Chapter 17: What Now? Practical Steps to Finding God in Chaos

I wrote a lot of this book while sitting in coffee shops with friends, discussing ideas, opinions, and personal stories about the ins and outs of suffering. We talked a lot about taking theology and making it practical. I like to think that you are reading this book as if we were having a coffee shop conversation. I hope that from beginning to end, it was practical in helping you shape a biblical worldview about suffering, a worldview that really does affect you on a day-to-day basis in your quiet time with God, in your conversations with friends, and in your part in fulfilling the Great Commission.

This last chapter is about taking practical steps to finding God in the midst of chaos. There's no magical formula to knowing God, but these are things that you can do as an aid to finding the much sought after peace in the storm.

Listening Prayer

I have been going to church since I was a baby, so I have heard a lot about prayer. Many times I was told that prayer is having a conversation with God. There's talking, and there's listening. But for a long time nobody taught me how to listen.

Part of listening to God means waiting for an answer to your prayers. That's important, yes, and He has taught me a lot about His character and His plan for my life through answering my prayers. It is always great when circumstances line up as, or better than, I prayed that they would. Another part of listening to God is reading the Bible while praying. It's almost unbelievable how much He will reveal to you if you are earnestly seeking Him and reading His Word.

There's also another aspect to hearing God's voice. It's when you find a quiet place, ask God questions, and wait to hear His response. When you hear from God, you know that He has not forgotten you. This isn't some form of divination; it's simply meeting with God and expecting Him to meet with you. A.W. Tozer said, "A word is a medium through which thoughts are expressed, and this application of the term to the eternal Son leads us to believe that self-expression is inherent in the Godhead, that God is forever seeking to speak Himself out to His creation. The whole Bible supports this idea. God is speaking. Not God spoke, but *God is speaking*. He is, by nature, continuously articulate. He fills the world with His speaking voice."[13] I would highly recommend the book *Can You Hear Me? Tuning in to the God Who Speaks* by Brad Jersak.

Personal Bible Study

While majoring in theology, one of the easiest traps for me to slip into was to focus on doing all the Bible reading for a class, and convince myself that I had "killed two birds with one stone." I did my homework and quiet time all at once. What I forgot was the importance of my intentional pursuit of the God I love through the reading of His Word. There is a huge difference between reading the Bible academically and immersing yourself in the Spirit as you intentionally and diligently seek Him.

Especially in times of turmoil, a great place to read the Bible is Psalms. David and the other psalmists wrote honestly and openly about feeling forsaken by God in the hour that they needed Him. When I am in distress, I find a psalm that resonates within me, and say it as a prayer. Another help is to go through a guided Bible study. Your church may have some resources.

Find Community

In times of suffering, it is tempting to let yourself become isolated. Don't! Acts 2:46 says, "Day by day continuing with one mind in the

13. Tozer, *The Pursuit of God*, 69.

temple, and breaking bread from house to house, they were taking their meals together with gladness and sincerity of heart." The importance of biblical community cannot be overstated. This doesn't just mean the weekly potluck at the Baptist church. True biblical community involves intentionally being with other believers, encouraging each other and being vulnerable.

Being with other believers is probably the best way to get out of a funk. And there is nothing like being with somebody who can say, "I know what it's like. I've been where you are." Opening up and sharing your pain and struggles with someone who understands, and letting them love you in that place of your pain, helps you understand that God also loves you in the place where you are.

Find Resources

Talk with your pastor, Sunday school leader, or trusted friend about solid books, sermons, or other resources on suffering. You just might find some of the answers that you were looking for. I highly recommend the book, *If God Is Good* by Randy Alcorn. *Boundaries: When to Say Yes, How to Say No to Take Control of Your Life* by Drs. Townsend and Cloud has been an invaluable resource for people who are trying to move on with their lives after a painful experience.

Stop Agreeing with Satan

Because of the cross, Satan's authority has been taken away from him. But when we agree with him, we re-empower a disempowered Devil. An agreement with Satan does not have to come in the form of voodoo or witchcraft. Every time we believe a lie about God or about ourselves, we are agreeing with the father of lies himself. The only way to combat Satan's lies is with truth. Confess the lies that you have been agreeing with, renounce them, and speak truth over your life daily, until truth becomes a living, breathing, walking reality in your everyday life. Here are some examples of lies from Satan, and the biblical truths that can set you free from them.

A Theology of Chaos

God has forgotten me. "Can a woman forget her nursing child and have no compassion on the son of her womb? Even these may forget, but *I will not forget you*. Behold, I have inscribed you on the palms of My hands; your walls are continually before Me" (Isaiah 49:15-16).

I am unloveable. "Who will separate us from the love of Christ? Will tribulation, or distress, or persecution, or famine, or nakedness, or peril, or sword? ...But in all these things we overwhelmingly conquer through Him who loved us. For I am convinced that neither death, nor life, nor angels, nor principalities, nor things present, nor things to come, nor powers, nor height, nor depth, nor any other created thing, will be able to separate us from the love of God, which is in Christ Jesus our Lord" (Romans 8:35,37-39).

This is the best that God has for me. "O afflicted one, storm-tossed, and not comforted, behold, I will set your stones in antimony, and your foundations I will lay in sapphires. Moreover, I will make your battlements of rubies, and your gates of crystal, and your entire wall of precious stones. All your sons will be taught of the Lord; and the well-being of your sons will be great. In righteousness you will be established; you will be far from oppression, for you will not fear; and from terror, for it will not come near you" (Isaiah 54:11-14). How is that for God's best?

I was a mistake. Psalms 139:13-16 says, "For You formed my inward parts; You wove me in my mother's womb. I will give thanks to You, for I am fearfully and wonderfully made; wonderful are Your works, and my soul knows it very well. My frame was not hidden from You, when I was made in secret, and skillfully wrought in the depths of the earth; Your eyes have seen my unformed substance; and in Your book were all written the days that were ordained for me, when as yet there was not one of them."

God can't/won't forgive me. Luke 7:36-50 tells the story of a prostitute who came into a Pharisee's house where Jesus was dining. She anointed His feet with expensive perfume and her tears, and wiped them with her hair. Jesus said that she loved much because she had been forgiven of many sins.

Inner Healing Ministries

Inner healing ministry, also known as prayer counseling, is similar to counseling, and even if you are already in counseling inner healing can be a great tool to help you find God in the midst of your suffering. Approaches may vary, but the general idea is to pray with a trained minister, asking the Holy Spirit to reveal the things in your life that are keeping you from enjoying communion with God. It can be any combination of lies from Satan that you are agreeing with, past hurts, and unforgiveness.

Seek a Quiet Place

A lot of you may be familiar with the "mountaintop experience," the "spiritual high," especially if you have ever attended youth camp or a churchwide revival. While it is great and wonderful to have a mountaintop experience, unfortunately it never lasts. You come down from the mountain back into the humdrum routines of daily life and either wonder where God went or wait for the next mountaintop experience. I have found that it is much more beneficial to seek moments of clarity instead. My friend has four young children, and I love spending time with them. But sometimes when I am called on to babysit, they drive me up one wall and down the other until I am ready to put all of them in bed at 4 p.m. But when we sit on the couch together to snuggle and read a book together or they color me a picture with nail polish and lipstick, I have a moment of clarity in which I remember how much I love them and why I love spending time with them.

I spent a year and a half living in Amman, Jordan, and let me tell you, it was not easy. My street was usually covered with diseased cats digging through trash; men gave me all kinds of grief on the streets; people back home promised me support but never sent it so I was always broke; and at one point my bank, which was located in America, got bought out so I was stranded in the Middle East without a working debit card. There were definitely days when I was ready to give up and go back home. But when I stood on my roof, from which I could see the whole city of four million people, I had moments of clarity in which I remembered how much I loved Amman, and that God really was going to take care of everything. Moments of clarity help remind me, at a heart level, of God's purposes and plans for my life.

It is just as important to seek places of rest. By rest, I don't just mean you go on vacation or catch up on sleep. I am referring to what the psalmist meant when he said, "Cease striving and know that I am God; I will be exalted among the nations, I will be exalted in the earth" (Psalms 46:10). I am talking about the kind of rest that God intended when He created the Sabbath and commanded the Israelites not to collect food on that day, because He would provide for them. Biblical rest is about knowing that God really is in control and taking care of everything, so we can relax and simply enjoy the fact that we are His.

Seek After Moves of God

The Christian community in Redding, California has been in a state of perpetual revival since the 1990s. Many people have moved to Redding for a short period of time, perhaps a year or two, to enjoy a season of rest in God's presence. One of the most powerful movements of the early 20th century was the Welsh Revival of 1904-1905. People travelled from mainland Europe and even North America to experience this movement of the Holy Spirit in Wales, in which hundreds of thousands of lives were changed. A hundred years later, people were travelling to the Brownsville Revival in Florida. Cecil and Suzanne both travelled there. Cecil says that he was blessed by the ministry, while Suzanne, who was in so much pain that she could barely walk, experienced complete physical healing.

Relocating or travelling thousands of miles may be a stretch for you. But maybe a man of God will be speaking or holding a conference in your area. Try to take advantage of it.

Forgive

This is probably the most important thing you can do in your pursuit of God, and it is also the most difficult. Many of you are probably familiar with the Lord's prayer.

"Our Father who is in heaven, hallowed be Your name. Your kingdom come. Your will be done, on earth as it is in heaven. Give us this day our daily bread. And forgive us our debts, as we also have forgiven our debtors. And do not lead us into temptation, but deliver us from evil. [For Yours is the kingdom and the power and the glory forever. Amen."] For if you forgive others for their transgressions, your heavenly Father will also forgive you. But if you do not forgive others, then your Father will not forgive your transgressions (Matthew 6:9-15).

Clearly forgiveness is crucial if we are earnestly seeking God. Whenever we release forgiveness to someone, we are releasing heaven's blessings over our own lives.

If it is too difficult for you to forgive your alcoholic father or the boss who fired you for no apparent reason, find somebody else who committed a lesser offense and whom you have a good relationship with to forgive. Then, when you begin to experience the joy of forgiving, it will be much easier to forgive the larger offenses.

Be Patient and Wait on God

Don't expect a quick fix or easy answers. God does rescue, but He truly delights in redeeming. He does have answers for you, and through practices like listening prayer, Bible study, and community He will reveal the answers you need as you are ready for them. You won't have all the answers or see the complete picture until you get to heaven though, so be patient. In Daniel 10, the prophet Daniel fasted for twenty-one days waiting for a response from God. In the end, the angel who had been sent to him with a message said that he was sent out on the first day of Daniel's fast, but he was detained by demonic forces.

When God answers your questions, it is never simply, "This happened to you for My glory," or, "This happened to you, of all people, because I knew that you could handle it." In John 9:1-7, Jesus and the disciples encountered a man who had been blind from birth. His disciples asked whose sin caused him to be born blind, and Jesus responded by saying that he was born blind so that the glory of God might be more fully revealed. But that wasn't His complete answer. His complete answer came when He healed the blind man. God gives heart answers that reveal more of Himself and His love for you, because what He really wants is not for you to be a theological whiz. What He really wants is for you to know Him and know how much He loves you.

Questions for Discussion/Reflection

1. Which of these steps would be most beneficial to you? Which ones are you not currently doing?

2. What are some more steps can you take, and encourage others to take, to find God in the midst of suffering?

3. Apart from those listed in this chapter, what are some of the lies of Satan that you have been believing? What biblical truths will break those lies?

4. Who do you need to forgive?

5. In what areas are you waiting on God?

About the Authors

Elysia McColley is the cofounder of Khubz-is-Samaa', an organization that helps refugees and orphans in the Middle East. She has been recognized for her insightful Bible teaching and has published many articles on social justice in the Middle East.

Email: Elysiamccolley@gmail.com

Website: www.elysiamccolley.com

Safhi Jai has traveled extensively throughout the 10/40 region. He has seen poverty, discrimination, and hopelessness at its worst. Safhi hopes to bring hope and change to the world through Christ.

More Titles by 5 Fold Media

The Transformed Life
by John R. Carter
$20.95
ISBN: 978-1-936578-40-5

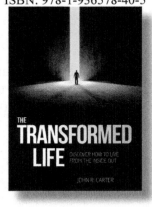

Personal transformation requires radical change, but your life will not transform until you change the way you think. Becoming a Christian ignites the process of transformation.

In this book, John Carter will teach you that God has designed a plan of genuine transformation for every person, one that goes far beyond the initial moment of salvation. More than a book, this 10 week, 40 day workbook will show you how to change.

Psalms: Poetry on Fire
The Passion Translation
by Brian Simmons
$19.00
ISBN: 978-1-936578-28-3

Now in Second Edition!

The ancient Psalms find the words that express our deepest and strongest emotions. They will turn your sighing into singing and your trouble into triumph. *The Passion Translation* of *The Psalms* will leave you amazed as the inspired words of Scripture unlock your heart to the wonder and glory of God's Word. It truly is *Poetry on Fire!*

I highly recommend this new Bible translation to everyone. ~ Dr. Ché Ahn, Senior Pastor of HRock Church in Pasadena, CA

Like 5 Fold Media on Facebook, follow us on Twitter!

"To Establish and Reveal"
For more information
visit:
www.5foldmedia.com

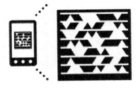

Use your mobile device to scan
the tag and visit our website.
Get the free app:
http://gettag.mobi